Laughter

ALL-TIME
FAVORITES

the Best
Medicine

Laughter
the Best
Medicine

ALL-TIME FAVORITES

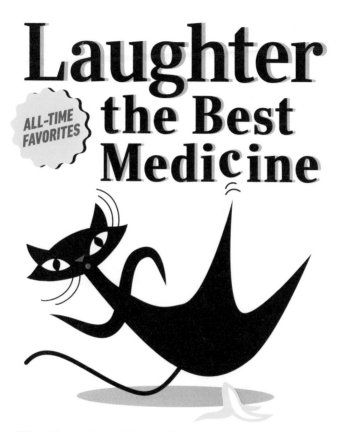

**The Funniest Jokes, Stories, and Cartoons
from 100 Years of *Reader's Digest***

Reader's Digest

New York/Montreal

A READER'S DIGEST BOOK
© **2022 Trusted Media Brands, Inc.**
44 South Broadway
White Plains, NY 10601

Cover illustration: Anna Beck

ISBN 978-1-62145-596-7 (paperback)
ISBN 978-1-62145-597-4 (e-pub)

We are committed to both the quality of our products and the service we provide
to our customers. We value your comments, so please feel free to contact us at
TMBBookTeam@TrustedMediaBrands.com.

For more Reader's Digest products and information, visit our website:
www.rd.com (in the United States)
www.readersdigest.ca (in Canada)

Printed in China
3 5 7 9 10 8 6 4 2

"Bit by the Fitbit" by David Sedaris, originally published in *The New Yorker,* currently collected in the book *Calypso* (Back Bay Books, 2018), copyright © 2018 by David Sedaris. Reprinted by permission of Hachette Book Group; *Reader's Digest,* June 2015

"Cricket Chirp Became an Earworm" by Nancy O'Connor, *Reminisce,* February/March 2019

"Early to Bed and Late to Rise" by Don Herold, *Reader's Digest,* August 1965

"Two Reveneurs Walk into a Bust" by Herman Fauss, *Reminisce,* December 2020/January 2021

"The Rest Stop Road Trip" by Mary Roach, *Reader's Digest,* June 2017

"Big Fish in Small Pond" by Bonnie Boerema, *Reminisce,* October/November 2020

"Excuse My Boo-Boo" by Corey Ford, *Reader's Digest,* June 1961

"Coming to Grips with a Sticky Situation" by Marianne Fosnow, *Reminisce,* April/May 2017

"Fast Track to a Dad Bod" by David Tate, *McSweeney's* (June 30, 2015), copyright © 2015 by David Tate; *Reader's Digest,* May 2016

"The Queen of Spin" by June Czarnezki, *Reminisce,* February/March 2021

"65 Million Women Want by Husband" by Erma Bombeck, from the book *Aunt Erma's Cope Book* (Fawcett, 1985), copyright 1979 by Erma Bombeck. Reprinted by permission of The Aaron M. Priest Literary Agency; *Reader's Digest,* May 1980

"Wardrobe Decision Leaves her in a Bind" by Rosemary Williams, *Reminisce,* April/May 2021

"The Great Pushball Incident" by Daniel V. Gallery, from the book *Clear the Decks* (William Morrow, 1951), copyright © 1951 by Daniel V. Gallery; *Reader's Digest,* June 1952

"Feeling the Heat" by Tom C. McKenny, *Reminisce,* August/ September 2019

"The Company We Keep" by John and Jean George, *The Christian Science Monitor* (December 15, 1958), copyright © 1958 by John and Jean George. Reprinted by permission of *The Christian Science Monitor; Reader's Digest,* January 1959

"The Dingoes Ate My Undies" by Jan Fenimore, *Reminisce,* October/November 2021

"A Moment with Mandy" by James Thurber, *Suburbia Today* (February, 1960), copyright © 1960 by James Thurber. Reprinted by permission of Barbara Hogensen Agency; *Reader's Digest,* April 1960

"The Housebreaker that Gave them the Slip" by Juda Woods-Hamlin, *Reminisce,* August/September 2018

"My Concession Speech" by Andy Simmons, *Reader's Digest,* October 2020

"She Saw Red and Lost It" by Maureen King Cassidy, *Reminisce,* August/September 2021

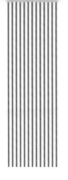

Contents

A NOTE FROM
THE EDITORS

It might seem hard to be funny for 100 years, but that's just what Reader's Digest has done since we first started sharing vhumorous stories back when we began publishing in 1922. Since then, our readers have shared their favorite funny moments through their contributions to Life in These United States, Laughter the Best Medicine, All in a Day's Work, and Humor in Uniform. These columns have provided balance to the magazine by showcasing just how amusing, comical, and laugh-out-loud funny everyday experiences can be.

Whether we are befuddled by the complexities of modern life, amused by an interaction with a coworker or a boss, chuckling over family foibles, or gobsmacked by the stupidity of our fellow humans, we come together to laugh at ourselves and with one another.

Sometimes we poke fun at the aging process to make it feel a little less daunting; maybe we joke about dating and relationships to take the sting out when they get hard or go awry. Even our military men and women share humorous stories of their time in service to our country, so that we might all find common ground. We laugh at the antics of animals and realize they aren't so different from us; we recognize the hilarity of a misunderstood word or a mixed-up communication; and we certainly know when something just bowls us over and makes us roll on the floor laughing.

In this volume you'll find the all-time favorites that we've discovered as we combed through the archives, all the way back to our beginnings. While some of the topics that made us laugh in the 1920s may feel a little dated now, the idea of sharing jokes and funny stories has been a hallmark of the magazine all along, and it continues to this day. Ultimately, readers share and enjoy what is funny about the human condition in all of its absurdity and authenticity.

Not only have we highlighted reader contributions, but we've also curated our favorite humorous quotable quotes, cartoons, and hilarious stories by famous writers that have appeared in the magazine. In "Bit by the Fitbit," David Sedaris warns of our lives being taken over by technology; in "65 Million Women Want My Husband," the legendary Erma Bombeck tries to put some romance back in her marriage, with hilarious results; and in "A Moment with Mandy," James Thurber becomes entrapped by an eight-year-old in a battle of wits, and barely emerges with his ego intact. These are just a few of the stories that have appeared in the magazine over the years, and we've brought them back because they have stood the test of time and continue to make us laugh all over again.

We hope that you'll treasure these jokes, cartoons, quotes, and stories as much as we do, and that you'll want to share our all-time favorites with your friends, family, neighbors, coworkers and maybe even the stranger on the train.

One hundred years later, we still believe that laughter is the best medicine, and we are thrilled to share this sidesplitting volume with you.

— **EDITORS OF** *READER'S DIGEST*

LIVING OUR BEST (FUNNIEST) LIFE

The first Sunday after my husband and I bought a new car, we parked it in the last row of the church lot, not wanting to be ostentatious. While talking with friends, my husband, Byron, accidentally hit the panic button on his electronic key. Immediately our car's horn blared and its lights flashed.

Watching Byron fumble with the button, his friend teased, "Wouldn't it have been in better taste to put a few lines in the church bulletin?"

— DONA A. MOWRY

Internet Humor
■

The most uncomfortable moment in my day is the time spent waiting in silence while someone searches for a "funny" YouTube clip I *need* to see.
— @EVAN_HADFIELD

When someone starts a Facebook post with "There are no words …" you'd better get prepared because you're about to read a lot of words.
— @JOSIEVORENKAMP

Yelp is a fun game where you try to guess between whether a restaurant is bad or a reviewer is crazy.
— @MIKEDRUCKER

To err is human; to point it out with glee is Internet.
— @APARNAPKIN (APARNA NANCHERLA)

I got stuck in a traffic jam while commuting into Los Angeles one day. The woman in the SUV in front of me took full advantage of the slowdown. She whipped out her eyebrow pencil, lip gloss, and a mirror, applying the finishing touches on her face in the ten minutes it took us to creep through the Cahuenga Pass.

Finally, the traffic broke up and as she zoomed away, I caught a glimpse of her vehicle's license plate: NTRL BTY.

— CHRIS DURMICK

My husband can't activate our Amazon Echo, because he keeps forgetting its name, Alexa.

"Just think of the car Lexus and add an 'A' at either end," I suggested. The next time he wanted to use our new toy, he looked a bit puzzled. Then he remembered what I'd said and confidently called out, "Acura!"

— LINDA PRICE

A few weeks back, I went to the hardware store and bought an ax to use on an overgrown shrub. I put the ax in a bag and went a few doors down to the grocery store, where I bought two bottles of wine. As the clerk placed the wine in the bag, he spotted the ax. "This," he said, "has all the makings of a very interesting weekend."

—LYLE BREWER

Service in the restaurant was abysmally slow. My husband was starting to flip out, so I tried to distract him with small talk.

"You know," I said, "our friend Christi should be having her baby anytime now."

"Really?" my husband snapped. "She wasn't even pregnant when we walked in here."

— MAUREEN MORRISON

I love the self-checkout aisle at my supermarket. The only problem comes when I leave an item on the scanner too long and the robo-voice scolds, "Please move your whole milk [or whatever] to the bagging area." Ordinarily, I just ignore it. But on my last shopping trip, I moved fast when the voice began shouting, "Please move your pork butt."

— LARRY MORETZ

I was visiting a friend who could not find her cordless phone. After several minutes of searching, her young daughter said, "You know what they should invent? A phone that stays connected to its base so it never gets lost."

— MIRIAM SKOW

When I stepped on the scale at my doctor's office, I was surprised to see that I weighed 144 pounds. "Why don't you just take off that last four?" I joked to the nurse's aide as she made a notation on my chart. A few moments later, my doctor came in and flipped through the chart.

"I see you've lost weight," he said. "You're down to 14 pounds."

— RACHEL WAGNER

During a visit to the ladies' room, my friend Addy heard the woman in the next stall suddenly ask, "So how are you?"

Startled, Addy replied tentatively, "Fine."

The woman then continued, "So what's new?"

Still confused, Addy said, "Not much. What's new with you?" It was then that the woman snapped, "Do you mind? I'm on the phone."

— MARION SPARER

Sitting at the kitchen table, I idly picked up a pack of cards and laid out a hand of solitaire, a game that I hadn't played in quite a while.

Having avoided the scale for a few years, my husband finally got up the nerve to climb aboard. Unable to read the numbers, he got off to grab his eyeglasses and stepped back on.

"What do you know?" he called out. "These glasses weigh fifty pounds."

— ERMA TIMPSON

My ten-year-old son came by and stopped to admire what I had done.

"Wow!" Zackary said. "You know how to play that without a computer!"

— SARAH NEVILLE

Friends and I were chatting over dinner in a restaurant. A man at the next table told his cell phone caller to hold on. Then he stepped outside to talk.

When he returned,

I said, "That was very thoughtful."

"I had no choice," he said to me. "You were making too much noise."

— NORM BLUMENTHAL

A solar-powered computer wristwatch, which is programmed to tell the time and date for 125 years, has a guarantee—for two years.

— DAILY MIRROR

A wife texts her husband on a frosty winter's morning: "Windows frozen!" Her husband texts back, "Pour lukewarm water over it." Five minutes later comes her reply: "Computer completely messed up now."

— CATHERINE HISCOX

I discovered a shortcut today. If you put your Fitbit in the dryer, you can get a head start on your steps. I had 3,800 steps in before I put on my pants!

— KATRINA HIGHTOWER

As a professor at Texas A&M, I taught during the day and did research at night. I would usually take a break around 9 p.m., however, calling up the strategy game Warcraft on the Internet and playing with an online team.

One night I was paired with a veteran of the game who was a master strategist. With him at the helm, our troops crushed opponent after opponent, and after six games we were undefeated. Suddenly, my fearless leader informed me his mom wanted him to go to bed.

"How old are you?" I typed.

"Twelve," he replied. "How old are you?"

Feeling my face redden, I answered, "Eight."

— TODD SAYRE, PH.D.

My family has a tradition of naming the cruise control on our cars. We were used to hearing my father proclaim "Take it, Max," as he flipped on the cruise control during long trips in our station wagon.

Recently, I was traveling with my parents in their new car when we hit a wide-open expanse of highway. My dad leaned back and said, "I think I'll let Tom drive for a while."

"Tom who?" I asked.

My mother translated for me: "Tom Cruise, of course."

— DANA MARGULIES

After my wife and I had navigated through a website for 20 minutes, a talking image of a woman popped up to offer help. "At last," my wife said, "a real person."

— VINCENT PALOZA

My friend is notorious for waiting until the needle is on empty before filling his gas tank.

I'd like the window that says "Are you sure you want to do this? OK/Cancel" to pop up less often on my computer and more in my real life.

— @AARONFULLERTON

Finally his car died on him, and we had to push it to the nearest filling station. After my friend finished pumping gas, the attendant asked if he had learned anything.

"Yeah," my friend muttered, "I learned I have a 15-gallon tank."

— EDWARD HYATT

was showing my kids an old rotary phone when my nine-year-old asked, "How did you text on it?"

My 15-year-old daughter roared with laughter, until a thought occurred to her: "Wait, where did you store your contacts?"

— TARA PRICE

recently bought a new car that had a faulty light. When, after five visits to the dealer's shop, they were unable to fix it, I tried to get it replaced by threatening to use my state's lemon laws.

My calls and letters to the dealer got me nowhere.

I went to a florist, ordered a fruit basket filled with lemons, and sent it to the dealer with this poem:

"When I drive my lemon, I'll be thinking of you.

"Pretty soon, my attorney will too."

A short time later the dealer called and asked what color I'd like my new car to be.

— JOHN T. CARROLL

BIT BY
THE FITBIT

An innocent fitness fad turns into a
seductive exercise in world domination.

By David Sedaris

I **was at an** Italian restaurant with a woman named Lesley. As she reached for an olive, I noticed a rubber bracelet on her left wrist. "Is that a watch?" I asked.

"No," she told me. "It's a Fitbit. You sync it with your computer, and it tracks your physical activity."

I leaned closer, and as she tapped the thickest part of it, a number of glowing dots rose to the surface and danced back and forth. "It's like a pedometer," she continued. "But updated, and better. The goal is to take 10,000 steps per day, and once you do, it vibrates."

I forked some salami into my mouth. "Hard?"

"No," she said. "It's just a tingle."

A few weeks later, I bought a Fitbit of my own and discovered what she was talking about. Ten thousand steps, I learned, amounts to a little more than four miles for someone

my size—five feet five inches. It sounds like a lot, but you can cover that distance in the course of an average day without even trying, especially if you have stairs in your house and a steady flow of people who regularly knock, wanting you to accept a package or give them directions or just listen patiently as they talk about birds, which happens from time to time when I'm home.

I was traveling myself when I got my Fitbit, and because the tingle feels so good, not just as a sensation but also as a mark of accomplishment, I began pacing the airport rather than doing what I normally do, which is sit in the waiting area, wondering which of the many people around me will die first, and of what. I also started taking the stairs instead of the escalator and avoiding the moving sidewalk.

"Every little bit helps," my old friend Dawn, who frequently eats lunch while Hula-Hooping, said. She had a Fitbit as well and swore by it. To people like Dawn and me, people who are obsessive to begin with, the Fitbit is a digital trainer, perpetually egging us on. During the first few weeks that I had it, I'd return to my hotel at the end of the day, and when I discovered that I'd taken a total of, say, 12,000 steps, I'd go out for another 3,000.

"But why?" my partner, Hugh, asked when I told him about it. "Why isn't 12,000 enough?"

"Because," I told him, "my Fitbit thinks I can do better."

Fitbit also helps satisfy my insane need for order at the same time. I've been cleaning the roads in my area for three years now, but before the Fitbit, I did it primarily on my bike and with my bare hands. That was fairly effective, but I wound up missing a lot. On foot, nothing escapes my attention: a potato chip bag stuffed into the hollow of a tree, an elderly mitten caught in the embrace of a blackberry bush, a mud-coated matchbook at the bottom of a ditch. You can tell where my territory ends and the rest of the nation begins.

Since getting my Fitbit, I've seen all kinds of things I wouldn't normally have come across. Once, it was a toffee-colored cow with two feet sticking out of her. I was rambling that afternoon with my friend Maja. As she ran to inform the farmer, I marched in place, envious of the extra steps she was getting in. Given all the time I've spent in the country, you'd think I might have seen a calf being born, but this was a first. The biggest surprise was how unfazed the expectant mother was. For a while, she lay on the grass, panting. Then she got up and began grazing, still with those feet sticking out.

"Really?" I said to her. "You can't go five minutes without eating?"

Around her were other cows, all of whom seemed blind to her condition.

"Do you think she knows there's a baby at the end of this?" I asked Maja after she'd returned. "A woman is told what's going to happen in the delivery room, but how does an animal interpret this pain?"

I thought of the first time I had a kidney stone. That was in New York, in 1991, back when I had no money or health insurance. All I knew was that I was hurting and couldn't afford to do anything about it. The night was spent moaning. Then I peed blood, followed by what looked like a piece of gravel from an aquarium.

What might I have thought if, after seven hours of unrelenting agony, a creature the size of a full-grown cougar emerged, inch by inch, and started hassling me for food?

> ## In recognition of all the rubbish I've collected, a garbage truck was named after me.

Was that what the cow was going through? Did she think she was dying, or had instinct somehow prepared her for this?

When I returned to the field several weeks later, I saw mother and child standing side by side, not in the loving way that I had imagined but more like strangers waiting for the post office to open. Other animals I've seen on my walks are foxes and rabbits. I've stumbled upon deer, stoats, a hedgehog, and more pheasants than I could count.

Back when Maja and I saw the cow, I was averaging 25,000 steps, or around ten and a half miles per day. Trousers that had grown too snug were suddenly loose again, and my face was looking a lot thinner. Then I

upped it to 30,000 steps and started moving farther afield. "We saw David in Arundel picking up a dead squirrel with his grabbers," the neighbors told Hugh. "We saw him outside Steyning rolling a tire down the side of the road"; "...in Pulborough dislodging a pair of Y-fronts from a tree branch." Before the Fitbit, I was in for the evening after dinner. Now, as soon as I'm finished with the dishes, I walk to the pub and back, a distance of 3,895 steps. There are no streetlights where we live, and the houses I pass at 11 p.m. are either dark or dimly lit. I often hear owls and the flapping of woodcocks disturbed by the beam of my flashlight.

I look back on the days when I averaged only 30,000 steps and think, Honestly, how lazy can you get? Now I'm up to 60,000, which is 25½ miles. Walking that distance at the age of 57, with completely flat feet and while lugging a heavy bag of garbage, takes close to nine hours—a big block of time, but hardly wasted. I listen to audiobooks and podcasts. I talk to people. I learn things: the fact, for example, that in the days of yore, peppercorns were sold individually and, because they were so valuable, to guard against theft, the people who packed them had to have their pockets sewed shut.

At the end of my first 60,000-step day, I staggered home with my flashlight, knowing that I'd advance to 65,000 and that there would be no end to it until my feet snap off at the ankles. Then it'll just be my jagged bones stabbing into the soft ground. Why is it some people can manage a thing like a Fitbit, while others go off the rails and allow it to rule, and perhaps even ruin, their lives?

While marching along the roadside, I often think of a TV show that I watched a few years back—*Obsessed*, it was called. One of the episodes was devoted to a woman who owned two treadmills and walked like a hamster on a wheel from the moment she got up until she went to bed. Her family would eat dinner, and she'd observe them from her vantage point beside the table, panting as she asked her children about their day. I knew that I was supposed to scoff at this woman, to be, at the very least, entertainingly disgusted, the way I am with the people on *Hoarders*, but instead I saw something of myself in her. Of course, she did her walking on a treadmill, where it served no greater purpose. So it's not like we're really that much alike. Is it?

In recognition of all the rubbish I've collected since getting my Fitbit, my local council named a garbage truck after me.

Then my Fitbit died. I was devastated when I tapped it and the little dots failed to appear. Yet I felt a great sense of freedom. It seemed that my life was now my own again. But was it? Walking 25 miles, or even running up the stairs and back, suddenly seemed pointless, since, without the steps being counted and registered, what use were they? I lasted five hours before I ordered a replacement, express delivery. It arrived the following afternoon, and my hands shook as I tore open the box. Ten minutes later, my new master strapped securely around my left wrist, I was out the door, racing, practically running, to make up for lost time.

"And, if you fall behind on payments,
it drives itself back to the dealership."

My husband was driving home from work when he was pulled over for not wearing a seat belt. Two days later—same ticket, same cop.

"So," the officer said, "have you learned anything?"

"Yes, I have," said my husband. "I've learned I need to take a different way home from work."

— **KIMBERLY OWEN**

I feel inadequate when talking with a mechanic, so when my vehicle started making a strange noise, I sought help from a friend. He drove the car around the block, listened carefully, then told me how to explain the difficulty when I went to get the repair.

Later at the shop I proudly recited, "The timing is off, and there are premature detonations, which may damage the valves."

"What are you doing?" my mother asked after I pressed several buttons on her microwave.

"Reheating these leftovers for two minutes at 80 percent."

"I didn't know you could do that."

"Sure. How do you reheat bacon?"

"Oh," she said, "that's two biscuits and a popcorn."

— **ROBIN ROBERSON**

As I smugly glanced over the mechanic's shoulder, I saw him write on his clipboard "Lady says it makes a funny noise."

— **KATE KELLOGG**

My husband, a professional computer-systems troubleshooter, rode with me in my new car one afternoon. He had been working on a customer's computer all morning and was still tense from the session. When I stopped for a traffic light, I made sure to leave a safe distance from the stop line to keep oncoming drivers from hitting the car.

I couldn't help but laugh when my husband impatiently waved at me to move the car forward while saying, "Scroll up, honey."

— **GEORGIA M. HARVEY**

I mentioned to my sons that some teens used Facebook to plan a robbery at a local shopping mall.

"How did the NSA miss that?" my 21-year-old asked.

"I told you guys," said my 17-year-old. "No one uses Facebook anymore."

— **MARY HEATHER REYNOLDS**

Three and a half agonizing hours at the Department of Motor Vehicles put me in a foul mood. I was still in a funk when I stopped at a store to buy a baseball bat for my son. "Cash or charge?" the young woman clerk asked.

"Cash," I snapped. Then I quickly apologized. "I'm sorry. I just spent half the day in line at the DMV."

"Would you like me to wrap the bat," she chirped, "or do you plan to go back?"

— ADRIEN D.

During a lesson, my driving instructor commented that he was seeing spots before his eyes. Deeply concerned, I told him how my father had suffered a detached retina a few years earlier and had complained of similar symptoms prior to diagnosis.

"This could be very serious," I said. "You must see a doctor immediately."

"Or you could just turn on the windshield wipers," replied the instructor.

— MARTIN ROSE

My friend and I were hitchhiking, but no one would stop. "Maybe it's our long hair," I joked. With that, my friend scrawled on a piece of cardboard: "Going to the barber." Within seconds we finally had our ride.

— VINCENT PALOZA

After we got broadband Internet, my husband decided to start paying bills online. This worked great; in fact all our bill companies accepted online payments except one—our Internet service provider.

— SARAH LIBERA

Timeless Humor from the '50s

■

The big electronic computer in the accounting department performed admirably until summer weather arrived. Then it practically quit.

A diagnosis of the trouble revealed that the machine was extremely sensitive to changes in temperature, so the only thing to do was to move it into an air-conditioned room.

Now, as we office drones perspire and droop, we are treated to the vision of the computer operating coolly and efficiently beyond the glass wall of its private office. What was that again about men being smarter than machines?

"The Wi-Fi password is
'buysomethingorgetout.'"

Overheard: "I hate talking cars. A voice out of nowhere says things like, 'Your door is ajar.' Why don't they say something useful, like 'There's a state trooper hiding behind that bush'?"

When shopping online, it's easy to forget that you may not be dealing with a large corporation.

I recently e-mailed a website asking why my purchases hadn't arrived, a week after I'd paid for them. Later the phone rang. "Sorry for the delay," said a teenager. "I'll check and get back to you. I can't get on my computer right now because my mother's vacuuming and this room only has one socket."

— TERESA HEWITT

I realized the impact of computers on my young son one evening when there was a dramatic sunset. Pointing to the western sky, David said, "I wish we could click and save that."

— THERESA KLEIN

Our doctor's office called to let my husband know that the results from his blood tests came back and he was just fine. That didn't suit him.

"What's my cholesterol?" he asked.

"Mr. Crocker, you are just fine," insisted the nurse.

"Still, I'd like you to mail me the results."

A few days later, he received a postcard from the doctor's office. It read, "Mr. Crocker, you are just fine!"

—CATHY CROCKER

While at the mall I passed two women, neither of whom looked particularly happy. Especially the one who said, "Nothing in my size fits me anymore."

—MARY WATERS

Timeless Humor from the '40s

■

The summer I was 12, an old New Hampshire farmer hired me to do chores.

He was perfectly content to live as his grandfather had lived before him, without newfangled contraptions, and never hurried for anything. One morning I was late and rode into his yard on my bicycle, pedaling furiously. "Well," he muttered disgustedly, "can't see no use in making your feet go as fast as you can just to give your rear end a ride."

— PFC. WALLACE G. ACKERMAN

*"You'll be relieved to hear your
phone's died too."*

THE GREAT THING ABOUT IDEAS IS THAT EVERY NEW IDEA LEADS TO TWO MORE … IDEAS BREED.

— JEFF BEZOS

We live in a society exquisitely dependent on science and technology, in which hardly anyone knows anything about science and technology.

— CARL SAGAN

Sometimes you lie in bed at night and you don't have a single thing to worry about. That always worries me!

— CHARLIE BROWN

Part of what makes a human being a human being is the imperfections. Like, you wouldn't give a robot my ears. You just wouldn't do that.

— WILL SMITH

Something very sad about the fact that I haven't read *Moby Dick*, but I have read the *Kindergarten Cop* Wikipedia page.

— AZIZ ANSARI

The more you find out about the world, the more opportunities there are to laugh at it.

— BILL NYE

If you don't have a crazy Facebook friend, you are the crazy Facebook friend.

— JIMMY KIMMEL

THE INTERNET IS JUST A WORLD PASSING NOTES AROUND A CLASSROOM.

— JON STEWART

CRICKET CHIRP BECAME A BAD EARWORM

It was a solo performance
they couldn't tune out.

By Nancy O'Connor

On the day my father left for a five-day conference, I rushed home from school to tell Mom that I finally understood long division. But she had something else on her mind. "A cricket must've hopped inside the piano," she said. "It's been driving me crazy."

I helped her lift the top of our antique Steinway grand, but we couldn't see the insect. Mom called the pet store to see if a cricket trap existed. It didn't, but the manager suggested luring ours with a bit of carrot. We went to bed hoping to find the intruder eating its breakfast the next day. In the morning, I did encounter the cricket—chirping inside the piano.

That afternoon, several neighbors stopped by to hear the one-note serenade. One put a stick in the Steinway, thinking the cricket could use it to crawl out. I kept watch,

but the cricket was a no-show.

Over the next few days, Mom retreated to the bedroom to escape that relentless chirping, and practically every neighbor on the street came by with different kinds of food to attract the insect.

When Dad came home at the end of the week, he took one look at us and asked, "Is something wrong?"

We related the Saga of the Cricket. As we spoke, my father leaned over the piano, at which point the stowaway, as if on cue, let out a peep.

Then Dad reached behind the Steinway and grabbed the smoke alarm on the wall. The thing chirped in what sounded like delight, while Mom and I stared in disbelief.

"It sounds like a cricket when it needs a new battery," Dad said.

Mom collapsed on the couch with a moan. "Wait until the neighbors hear about this."

WORKING
9 TO 5

After I sent out résumés to universities regarding faculty positions, my husband asked if I'd caught the typo—the one where I addressed the cover letter: "Dear Faulty Search Committee."

— JENNIFER GOLBECK

My buddy applied for a job as an insurance salesperson. Where the form requested "prior experience," he wrote "lifeguard." That was it. Nothing else.

"We're looking for someone who can not only sell insurance, but who can sell himself," said the hiring manager. "How does working as a lifeguard pertain to salesmanship?"

"I couldn't swim," my pal replied. He got the job.

— TEDD C. HUSTON

A human resources manager was going over one candidate's application. At the line saying "Sign here," the woman had written "Pisces."

— JAMES DENT

Catherine, a registered nurse, was unhappy with her job, so she submitted her resignation. She was sure she'd have no trouble finding a new position because of the nursing shortage in her area. She e-mailed cover letters to dozens of potential employers and attached her résumé to each one. Two weeks later, Catherine was dismayed and bewildered that she had not received even one request for an interview.

Finally she received a message from a prospective employer that explained the reason she hadn't heard from anyone else. It read: "Your résumé was not attached as stated. I do, however, want to thank you for the vegetable lasagna recipe."

— HARRIET BROWN

An enthusiastic young woman came into the nursing home where I work and filled out a job application. After she left, I read her form and had to admire her honesty. To the question "Why do you want to work here?" she had responded, "To get experience for a better job."

— DEBORAH L. BLAND

"More applicants from Monster.com!"

Job ad in the York, Pennsylvania, Daily Record: "Attention: Good hours, excellent pay, fun place to work, paid training, mean boss. Oh well, four out of five isn't bad."

This company has low standards and doesn't mind owning up. Its help-wanted ad: "Seeking laborers, equipment operators, and dumb truck drivers."

— CAROLYN CHEATHAM

Private school has a position open for science teacher. Must be certified or certifiable.

— THE DAYTONA BEACH NEWS-JOURNAL

I work at an aviation school that specializes in five-day refresher courses for aircraft mechanics. One day, I overheard a coworker talking on the phone with a potential customer. "Actually, we don't call our classes crash courses," he said.

"We like to think of them as 'keep up in the air' classes."

— RANDY G. SMITH

In the department store where I worked, my boss had asked me to look into hiring several cashiers. Reading through job applications, I burst out laughing at one answer. Next to the prompt "Salary expectations," the applicant had written a single word: "Yes."

— MICHEL PAYETTE

The employees' refrigerator at the graphic-design office where I work is notoriously messy. But I realized things were really getting out of hand when I saw an old jar of Vlasic-brand pickles that sported a new handwritten label: Jurassic Pickles.

— HOLLY SPRINGER

While working in the library at a university, I was often shocked by the excuses students would use to get out of paying their fees for overdue books.

One evening an older student returned two books that were way overdue and threw a fit over the "outrageous" $2 fee that I asked her to pay. I tried to explain how much she owed for each day, but she insisted she should be exempt.

"You don't understand," she blurted out. "I didn't even read them!"

— ALISON SATTERFIELD

Winding his way through the office cubicles, my son Mike spotted one of his employees playing a video game on the computer.

"Why aren't you working?" Mike asked him.

The employee had an excellent excuse: "I didn't see you coming."

— ROSEMARY SIEVE

Do you believe in life after death?" the boss asked one of his employees.

"Yes," replied the employee.

"That's OK then," said the boss. "Because while you were at your grandmother's funeral yesterday, she popped in to see you."

— GERALD MCDADE

My problem is getting to work on time. One morning, driving to the office, I came across a turtle in the middle of the road. I just had to rescue the creature. It took a few minutes for me to stop the car, grab the turtle, and move it off to the side. Then I rushed on to work.

When I saw my boss at the door, I said quickly, "It's not my fault, Rich. There was a turtle in the road." Before I could go any further he bellowed, "So what—you drove behind it?"

— CHRISTY STEINBRUNNER

Despite years of exceeding quota in my sales career, my lack of education was an obstacle whenever I searched for work. Finally, I started listing under "education" on my résumé, "College of Hard Knocks."

I was surprised, then, to be hired as regional sales manager by a Fortune 500 company that had required a degree in its job posting. Soon after I started, my boss came by and asked me, "So what was your major at the University of Knoxville?"

— JOE BOSCH

Timeless Humor from the '90s

■

Two fellows were relaxing after work and discussing a coworker's marital problems. "The good news," said one, "is that Fred's wife is seeing a therapist regularly. The bad news is that he's at the door as soon as Fred leaves for work."

— JOEY ADAMS

"You can call me dude or keep
the ponytail—pick one."

Only a few months before my father's retirement, the insurance company he worked for announced it would relocate to another state. He didn't want to move so late in his career, though, and the company was retaining ownership of the office building, so my father asked if he could stay on in some capacity.

The only available job, they told him, involved watering and caring for the building's many plants. Having little choice, my father trained with a horticulturist for a few weeks and then began his new work.

We worried about how Dad would cope with such a drastic change until he came home one day with new business cards. They read: "Raymond Gustafson, Plant Manager."

— ARLENE MORVAY

My wife and I were working at a furniture store liquidation sale. We were accepting fairly low bids, but one man proved a particularly tough customer. He pointed to a couch that originally cost $1,000, marked down to $300. "I'll give you $20 for it," he said.

"Sir," my wife replied calmly. "We are going out of business, not out of our minds."

— COLEMAN STOKES

I had an inkling I'd been working too hard at the gift shop when, at my father's funeral, I greeted all the well-wishers with, "Thank you. Come again."

— T. H.

Because I was processing my first accident report at the transport company where I worked, I was being particularly attentive. The driver had hit a deer on the highway, and the result was a severely damaged hood and fender. My serious mood was broken, however, when I reached the section of the report that asked, "Speed of other vehicle?"

The driver had put "Full gallop."

— DOUGLAS WAKEMAN

A big challenge of running a small business is dealing with employees' requests for time off. One morning an employee said, "I need to leave early tomorrow." Later that same day, he followed up with, "Looks like I'll be coming in late tomorrow, but if my coming in late runs into my leaving early, then I won't be in at all."

— JENNIFER KOONTZ

While in college I took a job in customer service at a department store.

One day a woman came in to complain about her billing statement. She was unhappy with our explanation, but paid her bill. Later, when I was reconciling the checks, I came across hers. She had written on the amount line, "Thirty-seven dollars and no sense."

— EDWARD A. LAMONT

The speaker at my bank's drive-through window had been broken for weeks, and we tellers had to resort to miming or writing notes to communicate with our frustrated customers. One day a sweet elderly lady whom I would see every week pulled up to the window, leaned out of her car and smacked the glass in front of my face.

"Hope this is bulletproof," she yelled.

There had just been a robbery at another bank nearby, so I was touched by her concern. "It is," I yelled back.

"Good," she continued, "because someone is going to shoot you if you don't get that speaker fixed."

— SARAH BANAKOWSKI

I was searching for the phone extension of a new employee who already had the reputation of being unpleasant. Striking out, I asked my coworkers, "Does anybody know Julie's extension?" A voice from the next cube over mumbled, "Try 666."

— MICHAEL BEST

Over the years I have heard my share of strange questions and silly comments from people who call the computer software company where I work as a tech support telephone operator. But one day I realized how absurd things can sound on the other end of the line when I heard myself say to one caller, "Yes, sir, you must first upgrade your download software in order to download our upgrade software."

— CARLOS MEJIA

Everyone at the company I worked for dressed up for Halloween. One fellow's costume stumped us. He simply wore slacks and a white T-shirt with a large 98.6 printed across the front in glitter. When someone finally asked what he was supposed to be, he replied, "I'm a temp."

— BRIAN DAVIS

"I wrote assembly instructions for children's toys. What did you do?"

EARLY TO BED AND LATE TO RISE

There are some mornings when it just doesn't pay to get out of bed—such as Monday through Friday.

By Don Herold

I've decided that getting up and going to work is just a form of nervousness, so I keep calm and stay in bed. It takes arrogance and courage, but I stay right there until I get some work done. Then I may go down to my office and play.

When I say play, I mean dictating letters, answering the telephone, holding "conferences," and doing those other office chores that most people call work.

I am an unusually energetic person, without a lazy bone in my body, and my natural impulses are to leap up, shave and dress in a jiffy, rush to the office, and start the day busily, achieving practically nothing. Instead I force myself to start what I consider real work at seven o'clock or eight, or whenever I wake up, and to stay at it and finish before I waste any pep on the useless, unimportant, conventional movements of rising and getting to an office, or distracting myself with the morning paper and the morning mail.

I never look at my mail until afternoon. Looking at the mail first thing is nothing but sheer boyish curiosity, mixed with a certain amount of laziness. A man who attends to his morning mail in the morning is letting others decide how he is to spend his day. (I've observed over the years that most people accomplish little more every day than getting up and going to work.)

My work is somewhat mental, and that a person can come nearer to being 100 percent mental in bed than anywhere else. His galluses don't chafe, his shoes don't hurt, the angle of the chair does not annoy him, and he does not have to figure what to do with his arms or legs. If he has a brain, he's practically nothing but brain ... in bed.

Another advantage is that bed is

the one place in the world where other people leave a man alone. People somehow regard bedrooms as sacred territory and do not, as a rule, crash in uninvited.

Furthermore, people feel that a man in bed fairly late in the morning must be sick, perhaps with something infectious. Let 'em think so!

Ruskin was grasping for a similar seclusion when he sent out cards reading: "Mr. J. Ruskin is about to begin a work of great importance and therefore begs that in reference to calls and correspondence you will consider him dead for the next two months."

Mark Twain was the patron saint of all bed workers. He was a sensationally sensible man, and he saw no point in getting up to write.

A more recent advocate of bed work was Winston Churchill, who remained in bed until late in the morning, then went to bed again after lunch and again later in the day. Thanks to this conservation of energy, he lived into his hearty 90s.

Another famous bed worker was Rossini, the composer. Once, while composing an opera in bed, he dropped one of the arias on the floor. Instead of getting up to retrieve it, he merely wrote a new aria.

It is said that Voltaire did most of his scribbling in bed, and that Disraeli wrote some of his greatest speeches while stretched out on the floor. And lawyer Louis Nizer said, "I prefer to work from a reclining position. Even my office chair tilts, and a hidden footrest permits me to recline sufficiently, without offending my client's notion of dignity. I have found justification for my lazy posture in medical journals that suggest that it takes strain off the heart and increases stamina as well as thinking powers."

My own theory is that an office is one of the least efficient inventions of modern man, and that it should be stayed out of as much as possible. If housewives only knew how most executive husbands frittered away their days, their awe of "father at the office" would become one more shattered schoolgirl illusion. Most men get more real work done on their trips and vacations than they do all the rest of the year.

My regimen of relaxation brings all sorts of shame on my head. I am called a laggard, a bum, an escapist. Perhaps I may even be accused of working for the Associated Mattress Manufacturers of America: If they can get everybody to spend 25 percent more time in bed, it will eventually boost mattress sales 25 percent. That's all right with me. What's good for them is good for the country.

When my printer's type began to grow faint, I called a local repair shop, where a friendly man informed me that the printer probably needed only to be cleaned. Because the store charged $50 for such cleanings, he told me, I might be better off reading the printer's manual and trying the job myself.

Pleasantly surprised by his candor, I asked, "Does your boss know that you discourage business?"

"Actually it's my boss's idea," the employee replied sheepishly. "We usually make more money on repairs if we let people try to fix things themselves first."

— MICHELLE R. ST. JAMES

I work in a small government office, and as part of the daily routine I take orders for doughnuts and pick them up on my morning run to the post office. A new employee looked bemused as I took orders for CCRs, GOFs and POFs—known to bakery staff as chocolate-covered raised, glazed old-fashioned, and plain old-fashioned. When it was the new employee's turn to order, she laughed and said, "You know you work in a government office when even the doughnuts have acronyms."

— CINDY BEVIN

As a new employee for a discount brokerage firm, I went for a month of classroom training. Warning us about the volume of information we were required to memorize, one instructor suggested we make lots of notes on index cards.

When I completed the course, I was assigned to a team where, as suggested, I taped all the cards, crammed with notes, onto my computer.

On my first day of trading, a veteran broker sat with me. He immediately noticed all the cards—and my apprehension—and promptly made up a new card, which he taped to my computer. It read "Breathe!"

— STEVE J. GAINES

I once had a boss tell me, "Don't dress for the job you have; dress for the job you want." I showed up the next day in a Cubs uniform.

— ROB PARAVONIAN

St. Peter: Why should I let you into Heaven?

Me: Once, a coworker said "supposably" seven times in a meeting, and I just let her.

St. Peter: Get in here.

— @ABBYCOHENWL

"If you want me to give 110 percent,
I want a 10 percent raise."

When I phoned my employee to find out why she hadn't come to the office, I expected to hear a sob story about how sick she was, blah, blah, blah. Instead, her excuse was pretty plausible. "When I was driving to work, I took a wrong turn," she explained. "And then I just decided to keep going."

— JUDIE SHEWELL

Anytime companies merge, employees worry about layoffs. When the company I work for was bought, I was no exception. My fears seemed justified when a photo of the newly merged staff appeared on the company's website with the following words underneath: "Updated daily."

— DIANNE STEVENS

Asked about the kind of job he wanted, an applicant at our tax management company stated, "I seek full authority but limited responsibility."

— MIKE WILKERSON

The young man loading groceries into my car let out a violent sneeze. "Bless you!" I shouted.

He leaned in the window, shook his head, and said, "Nah, just doin' my job. But thanks."

— D.L.

At the height of coronavirus chaos, our human resources director sat the employees down and explained the elaborate procedures for visitors coming to the locked front door of our business. "Visitors must ring the bell, sign in, be interrogated about their health, and not pass the inner entryway once inside," he said. Turning to one of my colleagues, he asked, "So what do you do when the doorbell rings?"

My colleague replied, "Go to the bathroom."

— SHERRY CAMPBELL

During a recent job search, I encountered many well-meaning human resources personnel. Often, if a position was filled, they sent letters to the other candidates informing them that someone else had been chosen. One especially empathetic human-resources manager wrote, "I'm sorry to say that we were able to find a candidate who fits our requirements."

— JOAN M. WEIS

My boss arrived at work in a brand-new Lamborghini. "Wow," I said. "That's an amazing car."

He replied, "If you work hard, put all your hours in, and strive for excellence, I'll get another one next year."

— BOREDPANDA.COM

In search of a new pastor, our congregation advertised for someone "able to walk on water and move mountains." We knew we had the right person when a candidate arrived for the job interview sporting a life jacket and carrying a shovel.

—MARJORIE KAUFMAN

Everyone knows I'm a stickler for good spelling. So when an associate e-mailed technical documents asking me to "decifer" them, I had to set him straight.

"Decipher is spelled with a ph, not an f," I wrote. "In case you've forgotten, spell-checker comes free with your Microsoft program."

A minute later came his reply: "Must be dephective."

— TERESA FISHER

Late one night I stopped at one of those 24-hour gas station mini-marts to get myself a fresh brewed cup of coffee. When I picked up the pot, I could not help noticing that the brew was as black as asphalt and just about as thick. "How old is the coffee you have here?" I asked the woman who was standing behind the store counter.

She shrugged. "I don't know. I've only been working here two weeks."

— PETER CULVER

I had prepared my son's résumé for a job application. I typed curriculum vitae at the top and his name underneath. He delivered the document to the company, and a week or so later, a letter came for him. The salutation read: "Dear Mr. Vitae."

—SHELAGH PRYKE

A customer brought her car into our Saturn dealership complaining of rattling noises. Later the technician said the problem was no big deal. "Just a case of CTIP: Customer Thinks it's a Porsche."

— ERIK DAVISON

*"I have to hang up now, I only have an hour
to get these reports done."*

Carpenters from California, Missouri, and New York showed up at the White House for a tour. The chief guard welcomed them with special enthusiasm because the front gates were in need of repair. He asked each person to come up with a bid. The California carpenter measured and figured and finally said, "Well, $400 for materials, $400 for my crew and $100 profit for me; $900 total." The guard nodded and turned to the carpenter from Missouri.

That man took out his tape measure and a pencil and, after some calculating, said, "It'll cost $700—$300 each for materials and my crew and $100 profit for me." The guard thanked the man and turned to the carpenter from New York.

Without hesitation, the New Yorker said, "This job will run $2,700."

The guard gasped. "You didn't even measure or do any calculating," he replied. "How do you figure it'll be so expensive?"

"Simple," said the New York carpenter. "$1,000 for me, $1,000 for you, and we hire the guy from Missouri."

— DAN ANDERSON

Our copier was on the fritz so I put a note on it: "Service has been called." When the technician told me he had to order parts, I added a second note: "Parts have been ordered."

During the next five days, when we had to use an older, slower copier on the other side of the building, someone taped a third note to the machine: "Prayers have been said."

— JENNIFER HARRISON

We Uber drivers never know whom we're going to end up with as a passenger. One day, I was driving over a new bridge, the design of which was very confusing. Completely confounded, I muttered, "I'd love to meet the genius who designed this mess."

With that, my passenger extended his hand in my

direction and said, "Well, today is your lucky day. My name is Mike, I work for the county engineer's office, and I'm the genius who designed this!" Surprisingly, he still gave me a tip.

— PATRICK GRILLIOT

I was interviewing a young woman who had applied for a job in our gift shop. It turned out that her favorite sport was soccer, and she was bending my ear about her accomplishments in the neighborhood league. Trying to steer the interview back to her job qualifications, I said, "Tell me about your long-range goals."

After thinking a minute, she replied, "Once I kicked the ball in from midfield."

— JENNIFER HARRISON

Following the announcement of an aggressive cost-cutting program at my company, each employee was encouraged to recommend ways to save money. A couple of days later, I stepped into an elevator where a large poster was hanging to remind workers of an upcoming blood drive. Underneath the huge words "Give Blood," someone had scribbled, "I knew it would come to this."

—CHUCK BRADFORD

My father still keeps the first dollar he ever made— and the police still keep the machine he made it with.

— NATALIA SKORUBSKI

My husband works for a high-tech company that uses a sophisticated robotic mail delivery system. The robot makes mail stops by following a clear painted line on the hallway floor. Recently the line had to be recharged with special paint. While it was drying, signs were posted warning, "Please don't step on the invisible line."

—JOELLEN BADIK

Timeless Humor from the '70s

■

My affluent neighbor was startled when her 14-year-old son announced that he wanted to become a garbage collector. "I'll never get used to that boy," she moaned. When I asked her why he should want to be a garbage collector, she sighed and said, "He thinks they only work on Tuesdays."

— JOAN D. LEE

IN THE BUSINESS WORLD, THE REARVIEW MIRROR IS ALWAYS CLEARER THAN THE WINDSHIELD.

— WARREN BUFFET

Work is a slice of your life. It's not a pizza.

— JACQUELYN MITCHARD

Beware of all enterprises that require new clothes.

— HENRY DAVID THROREAU

A professional is one who does his best work when he feels the least like working.

— FRANK LLOYD WRIGHT

Doing anything less than something amazing is squandering this whole reason that you're here.

— BRANDON STANTON

Don't stay in bed, unless you can make money in bed.

— GEORGE BURNS

A peacock that rests on his feathers is just another turkey.

— DOLLY PARTON

Oh, you hate your job? Why didn't you say so? There's a support group for that. It's called EVERYBODY, and they meet at the bar.

— DREW CAREY

CONFIDENCE IS 10 PERCENT HARD WORK AND 90 PERCENT DELUSION.

— TINA FEY

SO THESE TWO REVENUERS WALK INTO A BUST

New officer gets sobering lesson on working undercover.

By Herman Fauss

My friend Marvin Dunn, a new college graduate, reported for duty at the U.S. Bureau of Alcohol, Tobacco, Firearms and Explosives in Atlanta, Georgia. The ATF formed in 1972 and worked with state revenue agents, or revenuers, busting stills.

The ATF office in North Carolina was investigating a large-capacity still there. The local moonshiners knew all of the agents by sight, so the bureau hatched a plan to send young agent Dunn undercover to North Carolina to pose as a big buyer from Atlanta.

Asking around in North Carolina, Marvin soon found a bootlegger who would sell him all the moonshine he could haul. Marvin agreed to buy at least 500 gallons if he could examine the still to make sure it was safe and lead-free. Rather than lose such a large sale, the distiller agreed.

He took Marvin to the still, set up in an abandoned barn in the woods. Marvin approved the still and told the moonshiner he'd return with a truck the following night.

The agents met the next morning to plan the operation, using Marvin's map. When the bootleggers were loading the truck inside the barn, agents would surround it. At a flashlight signal from Marvin, the raid would begin, and Marvin would run away, with his covert identity intact.

The plan worked, except that in the commotion, a revenuer who had never met my friend grabbed Marvin, roughing him up.

"Stop! Don't you know who I am?" said Marvin. "I'm Dunn!"

"You're damn right, you're done!" the agent replied.

Years later, he and that agent, Jack Pomarance, met again in church. What a reunion, as they remembered the bust.

FAMILY FIRST

One morning my wife asked our four-year-old son, Jud, what he wanted for breakfast. "Soup," he said.

"Son, we don't eat soup for breakfast. We eat soup for lunch. So what would you like for breakfast?"

"Lunch," he replied.

— JON GOAD

Thanks to reruns, my kids discovered the old Ozzie and Harriet TV shows. My 11-year-old son was especially taken with Ricky Nelson. He wanted a guitar like his, wanted to sing like him, and decided to hunt down some of his old recordings.

After a long search he came home and announced, "I couldn't find any Ricky Nelson albums, so I got some made by his brother."

"David?" I asked, not recalling that he had much of a musical career.

"No. Willie."

— WENDY SILVEY

In fourth grade, my son had a huge crush on a classmate. So for Valentine's Day, he bought her a box of chocolates and took it into school. When I returned home from work, I found him on the couch eating the same box of candy.

"What happened?" I asked.

"Well, I thought about it for a long time," he said between chews. "And I decided that, for now, I still like candy more than girls."

— KYM LOKKEN

At the company water cooler, I bragged about my children's world travels: one son was teaching in Bolivia, another was working in southern Italy, and my daughter was completing a research project in India.

One coworker's quip, however, stopped me short. "What is it about you," he asked, "that makes your kids want to get so far away?"

— TODD W. KAISER

My favorite thing about watching a new movie with my five-year-old is probably watching it 17 times a day for the next three months.

— @THEBABYLADY7

I love making clothes for my five-year-old granddaughter. She seems happy to accept them. The other day I asked if she would like me to make her a skirt.

"Yes," she said. "But this time, could you make it look like it came from a store?"

— BONNIE LOGAN

My young son declared, "When I grow up, I'm going to marry you, Mommy."

"You can't marry your own mother," said his older sister.

"Then I'll marry you," he replied.

"You can't marry me either."

He looked confused, so I explained, "you can't marry someone in your own family."

"You mean I have to marry a total stranger?" he cried.

— PHYLLIS SHOWERS

Two letters arrived from my nine-year-old daughter, who was away at camp. One was addressed to Mom, the other to Dad. The sweet, short note to me said, "Dear Mom, I am having a lot of fun at camp. Tell Eddie [our cat] I miss him. I miss you. Love, Kenna." The even-shorter note she sent to her father: "Dear Dad, Read Mom's note. Love, Kenna."

— ROBIN HOLT

While my parents were painting their bedroom, my five-year-old sister walked in and asked, "What the hell are you doing?" Not realizing what she had said, she casually walked out.

After she left, my stunned dad then turned to my mother and asked, "Where the hell did she learn to talk like that?"

— MARJORIE ERICKSON

Timeless Humor from the '70s
■

A friend of mine was driving her seven-year-old son and a little girl to a party. She listened intently for conversation in the back seat, curious to hear her young son's attempts at polite talk. There was a long period of silence until finally the boy turned to his companion and asked, "Lost any teeth lately?"

— M. ROSTEN

When my eight-year-old asked how I knew I was pregnant, I told her that I had taken a pregnancy test.

"Oh," she said. "What questions were on the test?"

— LAUREL FALVO

In our busy household, meals had often consisted of frozen ready meals. Determined to give us a healthier diet, I decided to make a lamb casserole using fresh meat from the butcher, fresh vegetables from the greengrocer, and herbs from the garden. After hours in the kitchen, I served it up to an expectant family.

Everyone agreed the food was delicious. "It tastes so good, Mum," declared my son, "that if you hadn't told me you made it yourself, I'd have thought it was one of the frozen ready meals."

— LUCY GRACE

This is your great-grandma and great-grandpa," I told my grandson as I handed him a photo of my parents. "Do you think I look like them?" He shook his head. "Not yet."

— VERONICA DALE

Whoever said "Don't bite off more than you can chew" has never been to a buffet with my family.
@ATSUKOCOMEDY (ATSUKO OKATSUKA)

Even with a thousand games, dolls, and crafts to choose from, my customer at the toy store still couldn't find a thing for her grandson.

"Maybe a video or something educational?" I asked.

"No, that's not it," she said.

We wandered the aisles until something caught her eye: a laser gun with flashing lights and 15 different high-pitched sounds. "This is perfect," she said, beaming. "My daughter-in-law will hate it."

— MICHAEL TURNER

The downside to retirement, I told my daughter, a stay-at-home mom with three girls, is that you no longer feel euphoric about Fridays. "When you're retired, every day is Friday."

"I know what you mean," my daughter replied. "When you're a stay-at-home mom, every day is Monday."

— BRENDA JOULLIAN

I asked my brother-in-law, the father of four boys, "If you had it to do all over again, would you still have kids?"

"Yes," he said. "Just not these four."

— SHEILA LEE

My sister explained to my nephew how his voice would eventually change as he grew up. Tyler was exuberant at the prospect. "Cool!" he said. "I hope I get a German accent."

— STACI BAILEY

On his 18th birthday, my son announced that he was no longer obligated to observe the curfew we'd imposed on him.

"I'm 18," he announced. "And you can't stop me from leaving the house if and when I want to."

"You're right," I said. "I can't stop you from leaving. But I can stop you from coming back."

— PAUL ENNIS

A teenager brings her new boyfriend home to meet her parents. They're appalled by his haircut, his tattoos, his piercings. Later, the girl's mom says, "Dear, he doesn't seem to be a very nice boy."

"Oh, please, Mom!" says the daughter. "If he wasn't nice, would he be doing 500 hours of community service?"

— MARIA SALMON

Last Christmas morning, after all the presents were opened, it was clear that my five-year-old son wasn't thrilled with the ratio of toys to clothes he'd received. As he trudged slowly up the stairs, I called out, "Hey, where are you going?"

"To my room," he said, "to play with my new socks."

— RICK BURNS

Her class assignment was to interview an "old person" about his life, so my niece asked me, "What was the biggest historical event that happened during your childhood?"

"I'd have to say the moonwalk," I replied.

She looked disappointed. "That dance was so important to you?"

— JEAN ROSENSTEIN

Timeless Humor from the '60s

■

I was reading to my wife a newspaper report of the speech in which FCC chairman Newton N. Minow called television "a vast wasteland."

If you watch your TV set constantly, Minow had said, "you will see a procession of game shows, audience-participation shows, formula comedies about totally unbelievable families, blood and thunder, mayhem, violence, sadism ..."

My 12-year-old son, hearing part of the quotation, interrupted excitedly, "What time does that show go on, Dad?"

— ALLYN W. OWEN

"I see my kids' laundry."

My teenage niece, Elizabeth, was nervous as she took the wheel for her first driving lesson. As she was pulling out of the parking lot, the instructor said, "Turn left here. And don't forget to let the people behind you know what you're doing."

Elizabeth turned to the students sitting in the back seat and announced, "I'm going left."

— RACHEL NICHOLS

My oldest sister had made a salad for dinner and served it on everyone's plate before we sat down. Coming to the table, Dad caught my four-year-old sister, Amy, poking his salad and told her to stop.

Amy was very quiet all through dinner.

Finally, when the meal was over, Dad asked her, "Amy, why were you playing with my food?"

"I was trying to get the moth out," she replied.

— ANNA WOZNIAK

Since my 16-year-old son recently received a prepaid cellphone as a gift, I've asked him to use it to call home if he's out past his curfew. One Saturday while waiting up for him, I dozed off in front of the TV.

Later, I woke to realize that there was no sign of him and no call. Irate, I punched in his number. When he answered I demanded, "Where are you, and why haven't you bothered to phone?"

"Dad," he sleepily replied, "I'm upstairs in bed. I've been home for an hour."

— DON JENTLESON

I had never been so zonked in my life. After my first child, Amanda, was born, my mother came to stay with me for a few weeks to help out, but I still woke up whenever the baby made the slightest sound during the night. One morning, I groggily asked my mom, "How long before I stop hearing every noise Amanda makes?"

Mom was obviously only half-listening. "Honey, are you coming down with something?" she asked. "You were coughing in your sleep."

— CAROL HERLONG

Spotted on a bumper sticker:
"I'm not a brat. Am not, am not, am not!"
— JACQUELINE PORTER

This teenager was in my boutique for at least an hour choosing the perfect dress for a party. But the next day she was back with the outfit.

"Can I exchange this for something else?" she asked.

I was surprised, but I couldn't argue with her explanation: "My parents like it."

— SALI THOMAS

On one occasion while my niece Lupita was in preschool, in our eagerness to help her remember what it was she had learned during the week, my sister wrote the symbol "+" on a piece of paper and asked the girl: "What sign is this?"

"It's a plus," she responded.

"And what is it used for?" we asked.

With an air of independence, she answered: "Well, it's for turning up the volume on the television!"

— MARTHA CUATECONTZI XOCHITIOTZI

No one is more cautious than a first-time parent. After our daughter was big enough to ride on the back of my bicycle, I bought a special carrier with a seat belt and got her a little helmet. The day of the first ride I put her in the seat, double-checked all the equipment, wheeled the bike to the end of the driveway, carefully looked both ways and, swinging my leg up over the crossbar, accidentally kicked her in the chin.

— ZACHARY GIBBS

Parenthood
■

I like having conversations with kids. Grown-ups never ask me what my third-favorite reptile is.
@SIMONCHOLLAND

My two-year-old has a superpower: Everything he touches gets sticky.
@A_PANIAGUA

We could live inside the school bus and my son would still find a way to make us late for it every day.
@DADANDBURIED

THE REST STOP ROAD TRIP

As the saying goes, "Not one bladder
empties but another fills."

By Mary Roach

family is a collection of people who share the same genes but cannot agree on a place to pull over for lunch. Ed and I, plus his parents and sister Doris, and eight-year-old niece Alisha, are on a road trip to Yosemite. Poppy wants Subway, Ed wants In-N-Out Burger, and Mary wants Sonic. In the end, we compromise on McDonald's, where Alisha will get an action figure that will come in handy later for breaking the heater vent of our rented minivan.

It's a three-hour drive to Yosemite, but we're taking a little longer, as we're working in a tour of Highway 80's public restrooms. As the saying goes, "Not one bladder empties but another fills." I am reminded of that track-and-field event wherein one person runs for a while and then hands off the restroom key to the next person, who runs until she's done, and then another person runs. Unhappily, many of these restrooms belong to gas stations. Gas station customers, perhaps inspired by the nozzles on the pumps outside, are prone to dribble and slosh. Though I almost prefer this to the high-tech humiliation of air travel, where the toilets flush mere seconds after you sit down. It's like having your plate cleared before you've even salted your potatoes.

We get back on the road. Poppy's driving now. We've entered the road trip doldrums, the point when all the cheesy tabloids have been read, the travel Etch A Sketch has grown boring, and anyone under age 12 is required to say "Are we there yet?" at ever-shortening intervals. Ed and his sister, two middle-aged adults, are playing with the highway bingo set. Alisha is making her action figure fight with Poppy's earlobes. Doris covers the bingo square that says motel. "Bingo!" "No way," says Ed. "A motel is only one story high and has a swimming pool full of algae. That was a hotel." "Same diff," says Doris. "Ma! Doris is cheating!" Alisha kicks the back of Poppy's seat. "Are we there yet?" If by there she means the end of our rope, then, yes, we're pulling in right now.

Just outside Manteca, California, we stop for coffee. Coffee is an important feature of the restroom-relay regimen. Without it, the chain could be broken, the gold medal lost. At a Starbucks checkout, Ed buys a CD of Joni Mitchell's favorite musical picks. The hope is that it will have a calming effect. The first cut is by Duke Ellington. Alisha makes a face. "It's not my favorite Ellington number," agrees Nana. The CD returns to its case, pending the day Joni Mitchell joins us on our annual vacation.

As we pull back onto the highway, it starts to pour, which at least quells the debate over whether to have the windows open. Depending on whom you ask, the temperature inside the minivan is either "freezing" or "so hot I'm going to suffocate."

Then something amazing happens. As we climb the Sierras, the rain turns to snow. The pines are flecked with white. We're struck dumb by the scene outside. For a solid 15 minutes, everyone forgets about their bladder, their blood sugar, the temperature in the van. Alisha has never seen snow, so we pull over to make snow angels and catch falling flakes on our tongues. Then Ed realizes we need tire chains, and we have to turn back and drive 30 miles to Oakhurst. "Good," says Poppy. "There was a very nice restroom there."

"What kind of parents let their children get tattoos?"

He was doomed to fail, but last Easter, my husband tried unsuccessfully to get our young sons to have some lunch after they'd already stuffed themselves with a ton of chocolate eggs.

"They're not going to eat," my mother-in-law told him. "It's Easter Sunday. What do you expect, a miracle?"

— JENNIFER SMITH

En route to Atlanta, my stepfather spotted some mules by the side of the road. "Relatives?" he asked my mother.

Not taking the bait, she responded, "Yeah, through marriage."

— ERICA VANNOY

While texting with my brother about our family vacation plans, I expressed concern regarding my asthma and the fact that he lives at such a high elevation. But autocorrect sent this: "We have talked about coming to visit you, but between my asthma and your attitude, I'm not sure if that will be possible."

— SUSAN FINNEGAN

Uncle Bart was a city boy whose familiarity with wildlife began and ended with pigeons. One time he joined us at our cabin in the woods. In the evening, he opened the door to let our cats in. The first cat walked in; then the second. Bart stood there coaxing the third cat to come, which we found strange—we had only two cats. The third cat was a possum.

— JONATHAN HAKULIN

My preteen daughter and I were out shopping. I called her over to where I was, and she responded with the same thing she always said whenever I needed her for something: "Just a sec!"

I didn't even think before I called back, "No more secs for you, young lady. Get over here right now!" Big oops as soon as it left my mouth and I noticed that people had turned around to stare at us.

— BONNIE SKINNER

During Thanksgiving dinner last year, my eight-year-old son watched intently as my husband carved the turkey. "Man," he said in awe. "They must have fed bread to that turkey for months to get all that stuffing."

— HEATHER JOHNSON

What's the difference between an outlaw and an in-law? Outlaws are wanted.

A mother gave her grown son two sweaters for Hanukkah. The next time he visited, he made sure to wear one. As he entered her home, instead of the expected smile, she frowned. "What's the matter?" she asked. "You didn't like the other one?"

— JENNIFER PAULY

When our son Patrick was four, we still marked all his Christmas presents "From Santa Claus." A couple of hours after he opened them on Christmas Day, I noticed that he seemed quite glum, for no apparent reason. "What's the matter?"

"Well," said Patrick. Long pause. "Well, I really thought you and Mommy would give me something for Christmas."

— ALEXANDER FARRELL

Our family was dazzled by the sights and the bustling crowds during a visit to Manhattan. "This is the city that never sleeps," I told my 11-year-old daughter.

"That's probably because there's a Starbucks on every corner," she observed.

— LINDA FOLEY

I was thrilled to be moving into my own house, even though it was only a block away from my parents' home. The very first morning on my own I relaxed on the porch and listened to some music, enjoying my new independence.

Then the phone rang. It was my father telling me to turn the sound system down.

— ELI STICKLER

For serving as flower girl for her aunt, three-year-old Sydney received a doll and bridal-themed gifts. Sydney was so thrilled, she ran to her aunt and announced, "I want this for all your weddings!"

— HELEN THOEN

To save money, I suggested to one of my grown sons that we all live together in one house. I could tell he didn't think it would be cost-effective when he asked, "Who's going to pay the therapist?"

— VIRGINIA DAVIES

"Thanks for the talk, Dad. But I was asking about the birds and bees for my zoology test."

Sometimes my mother would surprise us by visiting our house on Sundays after Mass. I was a busy mom with my own business and six children still at home. Housework was not at the top of my to-do list. One Sunday, my adult son, Dan, was also visiting. When Mom remarked that she hadn't yet seen his apartment, he told her to let him know when she would like to see it so he could clean.

"I'd be embarrassed to have you just drop by," Dan said. "It can be a real mess."

"Worse than this?" she blurted.

— **MARY POTTER KENYO**

"He's outside setting up a tent for the kids."

When my brother, my sister, and I were little kids and we ran around outdoors, my mom would say, "If you fall down and break your legs, don't come running to me!"

— KATHY MILICI

After the Halloween rush at my parents' costume business, we discovered that we had many clown noses left unsold. My mom decided to set up a sale box on the counter, hoping they'd move a little faster. And they did, after she put a sign over the box that read: "Pick your nose here!"

— PAULINE KINGSMAN

On our way to my parents' house for dinner one evening, I glanced over at my 15-year-old daughter. "Isn't that skirt a bit short?" I asked. She rolled her eyes at my comment and gave me one of those "Oh, Mom" looks.

When we arrived at my folks' place, my mother greeted us at the door, hugged my daughter, then turned to me and said, "Elizabeth! Don't you think that blouse is awfully low-cut?"

— ELIZABETH SCOTT

An elderly gentleman with a hearing problem goes to an audiologist, who fits him with hearing aids. A month later, the man returns to the doctor for a checkup. "Your hearing is almost perfect," the doctor remarks. "Your family must be really pleased you can hear again."

"Oh, I haven't told them yet," the gentleman replies, "I just sit around and listen to their conversations. I've changed my will three times so far!"

— ROY THIRWELL WARNER

My two sons, Jake and Austin, are a handful. So I wasn't surprised that my dad looked frazzled after we took them to a football game.

"It will be a cold day in #@%* before we come to another game," he muttered.

"Did you hear that?" Jake shouted to Austin. "Grandpa's going to take us to a game in December!"

— DREW SPECHT

Our family took hours to set up camp on a recent outing. But the couple and three kids who pulled up next to us did it in mere minutes.

"How did you manage that?" I asked the father.

"I have a system," he said. "No one goes to the bathroom until everything is set up."

— ARI ROSNER

THE PERFECT PARENT IS A PERSON WITH EXCELLENT CHILD-REARING THEORIES AND NO ACTUAL CHILDREN.

— DAVE BARRY

Madam, there's no such thing as a tough child—if you parboil them first for seven hours, they always come out tender.

— W.C. FIELDS

When my daughter was born, we videotaped the birth. Now when she makes me angry, I just hit "rewind" and put her back in.

— GRACE WHITE

Having a baby is like getting a tattoo on your face. You really need to be certain it's what you want before you commit.

— ELIZABETH GILBERT

The other night I ate at a real nice family restaurant. Every table had an argument going.

— GEORGE CARLIN

My perspective on my mother has changed immensely. She was a lot taller when I was younger.

— HOWIE MANDEL

There's no love without loss. It's a package deal.

— BRAD PITT

FRIENDS ARE GOD'S WAY OF APOLOGIZING TO US FOR OUR FAMILIES.

— ANONYMOUS

BIG FISH IN A SMALL POND

Little brother fell for it
hook, line and sinker.

By **Bonnie Boerema**

This is a different kind of fish story, one that's really about the relationship between two brothers. The younger one, Butch, is easygoing and dedicated. Kenny, who's my husband, is seven years older and has always been a joker. He loves to play tricks, especially on his little brother.

For his fifth birthday, Butch got an aquarium. It was filled with aquarium ornaments and had a lot of room for several small goldfish to swim. Every day after school, like clockwork, Butch fed the little guys. He loved those fish.

This routine went on for some time, until Kenny had the bright idea of playing a prank on his little brother. One day, Kenny bought a large goldfish—about 6 inches—and used Butch's fish net to move all the little goldfish from the aquarium into a smaller bowl. He left the one big fish in the aquarium. (It was a good thing Butch was taking a particularly long time returning from school that day.) Then Kenny hid in his brother's closet and waited.

The first thing Kenny heard after his brother got home was Butch yelling, "Mom! Look!"

Their mom came in and was as flabbergasted as Butch at the surprise in the aquarium.

Kenny listened to Butch trying to account for the mystery: "Maybe I mixed the fish food, and I discovered something. I could be rich!" Mom wondered where the other fish were, and Butch surmised that the big goldfish had eaten the little ones.

Finally, Kenny couldn't contain himself, and he came out of the closet, laughing so hard tears were falling. The jig was up.

As usual, Kenny got in trouble, but he was used to that.

DUMBING DOWN

The first day at my new health club, I asked the girl at the front desk, "I like to exercise after work. What are your hours?" "Our club is open 24/7," she told me excitedly, "Monday through Saturday."

— APRYL CAVENDER

When I was in the sixth grade, I lost the sight in my right eye during a playground mishap. Fortunately, the accident had little effect on my life. When I reached my 40s, however, I needed to get glasses.

At the optometrist's office, the doctor's young assistant pointed to an eye chart. "Cover your right eye and read line three," she said.

"I'm blind in my right eye," I told her. "It's a glass eye."

"OK," she responded. "In that case, cover your left eye."

— BILL SLACK

Larry wins the lottery and dashes downtown to claim his prize. "Give me my $20 million," he tells the man in charge.

"Sorry, but it doesn't work that way," the man says. "You'll get a million today, and then the rest will be spread out over the next 19 years."

Larry is furious. "Look, I want my money! And if you're not going to give me my $20 million right now, then I want my dollar back!"

— MIKE BROWNING

After hearing stories about radioactivity in granite countertops, my wife became alarmed.

"I have granite in my kitchen," she told a friend.

"Maybe you should get a Geiger counter," her friend suggested.

My wife was intrigued. "Are those the granite imitations they sell at Costco?"

— DANIEL OSTER

My friend was working at an amusement park when a couple stopped him. "Excuse me," said the woman, pointing to a pond. "What is that water made out of?"

Bemused, my friend replied, "Two parts hydrogen and one part oxygen."

"See?" she said to her boyfriend. "I told you it wasn't real."

— AMELIA WINES

I **walked** into the lobby of my apartment building recently and was greeted by this notice: "To whoever is watering these plants, please stop. They are the property of the building, and our maintenance staff will take care of them. They may have already been watered, in which case you will be overwatering them. Besides, these plants are fake."

— PAUL ROGERS

S **hopping** for deodorant, my daughter picked one up and read the label: "Dermatologist Tested."

"Good," she said. "They're no longer testing it on rabbits."

— LYNN CARROLL

I **sold an** item through eBay but it got lost in the mail. So I stopped by my local post office and asked them to track it down.

"It's not that simple," the clerk scolded. "You have to fill out a mail-loss form before we can initiate a search."

"OK," I said. "I'll take one."

He rummaged under his counter, then went to some other clerks who did the same—only to return and confess, "You'll have to come back later. We can't find the forms."

— DOREEN L. ROGERS

C **alling for** information about one of my credit cards, I got the following recorded prompt: "Please enter your account number as it appears on your card or statement."

I did as instructed, and the system said, "Please enter your five-digit ZIP code."

After I put that in, I got a third message: "If you would like your information in English, press one."

— MICHELLE GOLF

Timeless Humor from the '70s

■

In reviewing the academic record of one of my students so that I could write her a letter of recommendation, I noticed that among many good grades she had also earned an F. Since she had achieved high grades in difficult subjects such as physics and philosophy, the F in a physical education course seemed peculiar. "How did you manage to get an F in archery?" I asked. She looked sheepish and replied, "I shot the teacher."

— M. B. M.

I was struggling to separate one shopping cart from another at the supermarket when a fellow customer came to my aid.

"It seems to be shopping cart mating season," I joked.

"I certainly hope so," she said, tugging on one. "They never have enough carts at this store."

— MARJORIE KNOWLES

I answer a lot of questions at the information desk at Olympic National Park, in Washington state. But one visitor stumped me: "Do you have any trails that just go downhill?"

— MIKE PERZEL

My scrupulously honest husband caught a coworker helping herself to company trash bags and called her on it. "So what?" she argued. "They're just going to throw them away."

— PATRICIA HUTCHENS

Escape rooms are a popular craze in which participants solve puzzles and clues to free themselves from a locked room. Many people find them fun, but not one

"There's nothing wrong with your eyesight. You're wearing your seatbelt too high!"

burglar in Vancouver, Washington. He broke into an escape room after hours and became trapped. He eventually figured out how to leave. He called 911.

— RAVEMOBILESAFETY .COM

I used to drive an Eclipse. I think it was a nice car, but I couldn't look directly at it.

— BUZZ NUTLEY

While prosecuting a robbery case, I conducted an interview with the arresting officer. My first question: "Did you see the defendant at the scene?"

"Yes, from a block away," the officer answered.

"Was the area well lit?"

"No. It was pretty dark."

"Then how could you identify the defendant?" I asked, concerned.

Looking at me as if I were nuts, he answered, "I'd recognize my cousin anywhere."

— MORRISON LEWIS JR.

A fellow is having computer problems at work, so he calls the IT department. A technician arrives and asks the man for his password.

"My password is *MickeyMinnieGoofy-PlutoHueyDewey LouieDonaldBerlin*," the fellow replies.

"Why is it so long?" the technician asks.

"Because," the man replies, "I was told it had to be eight characters and a capital."

— PETER ROGERS

Last fall, a vacationer called to make a reservation at my campground. But first, she had a question: "Can you tell me what day the leaves change color?"

— PAMELA BROWN

A friend of ours was puzzled with the odd messages left on his answering machine. Day after day, friends and family would talk and then say, "Beep." He discovered the reason for the joke when he decided to listen to his greeting.

"Hi," it said. "I'm not in right now, so please leave a beep after the message."

— SHEEBA MATHEW

During a stickup, a bank robber in Phoenix, Arizona, told the teller to hand over "all the twenties, forties, and sixties."

— *PHOENIX TIMES-HERALD*

© Jon Carter • cartertoons.com

The front office asked us to figure out the square footage dedicated to each department in our clothing store. To save time, I suggested we count the ceiling tiles above each department.

"They're each two square feet. Counting the tiles would give us an accurate dimension of each department without having to work around all the displays," I explained.

My boss hated the idea. "Hell-ooo," she said, sarcastically. "We need the square footage of the floor, not the ceiling."

— TERRI HANKE

I asked a man on a country road for directions to a friend's house. "Go straight up the road till you reach the place where the barn burned down," he said. "Make a right onto the dirt road till you see a shed with a dog out front, and then make another right and continue up a mile."

"What if the dog isn't out front?" I asked. Perplexed, he said, "Make a right, anyway."

— KAREN HENRY

When I took my school-age daughters to a lunch with veterans, I told them to ask questions.

One of the men said he'd fought in the Korean War, and the girls were so impressed that the eldest wanted to know more: "Did you fight for the North or the South?"

— LETHA SCRIMPSHER

With talk of downsizing the United States Postal Service always in the air, our union steward passed the word to all the letter carriers that we needed to be proactive.

"Save our jobs," he urged. "E-mail your congressman."

— SUSAN KEMP

I had ordered vanity plates to go with my very first car. But instead of getting a pair, as I expected, I thought I'd only been sent a single plate.

But I forged proudly ahead with the plate installation, and when I finished, my father came outside and asked, "Why'd you put on only one?"

"That's all the state sent me," I replied.

"Is that right?" Dad said with a grin. Kneeling down, he undid the screws, slid a fingernail along the edge of the plate, and popped off a second one.

The name on my personal plates? "DITZ E 2."

— MICHELLE APOSTOULADIOS

The man sitting next to me on a recent flight was terrified of planes; he couldn't stop shaking. So I suggested he get a Scotch from the flight attendant, which he did, drinking it down in one gulp.

"Can I get another one?" he asked me. I pointed out the button above his head and told him to press it if he wanted another drink.

He promptly stood up, pushed the button, and held his glass underneath it.

— ROBERT NURTON

on. One woman looked rather glum.

When the leader asked why, she replied, "Well, I've done my best to stick to the diet plan, but I've had real difficulty. Try as I might, I just can't drink 68 glasses of water a day. All I can manage is 46."

— GILLIAN FRANCE

Does anyone in this room need to be dismissed from jury duty?" my father, a judge, asked a roomful of prospective jurors.

A nervous young man stood up. "I'd like to be dismissed," he said. "And why is that?" "My wife is about to conceive." Slightly taken aback, Dad responded, "I believe, sir, you mean deliver. But either way, I agree. You should be there."

— BETH DUNCAN

While searching for murder suspect Sterling F. Wolfname, cops in Billings, Montana, ran into someone at

My mother joined a new Weight Watchers group. At the first session, the group leader explained the healthy-eating plans everyone should follow, including drinking six to eight glasses of water a day.

The following week, the leader asked how everyone was getting

Timeless Humor from the '30s

■

A book agent once called on president Lincoln and sought to sell him a book for which he had no use. Failing, he asked Lincoln if he would not write an endorsement of the work, which would enable him to sell it to others. Whereupon the President, always anxious to oblige, with a humor entirely his own, wrote: "Anyone who likes this kind of book will find it just the kind of book he likes."

— ELLEN HARBOLD

"I'm afraid of the dark, so could I get one with a night-light?"

a shelter who matched his description. When they asked him if he was Wolfname, the man said he wasn't. The officers concluded he was fibbing when they spotted this tattoo on his head: *Wolfname*.

— READER'S DIGEST

While working on a new house one day, I overheard two carpenters talking.

"Check it out," one of them said, pointing to the leaden sky. "Some ominous clouds are headed our way."

"No way," came the reply. "Those are cumulus."

— GEORGE BUTLER

When I asked my friend if she was planning to attend church, she just shook her head. "I haven't gone in a long time,"

she said. "Besides, it's too late for me. I've probably already broken all seven commandments."

— NANDIARA HENTGES

I wish I had enough money to buy an elephant."

"What on earth do you need an elephant for?"

"I don't. I just need the money."

— SAM LEVENSON

EXCUSE MY BOO-BOO

An expert bungler details his journeys
through blooper land.

By Corey Ford

I **can remember** names if I don't have to. It's when the pressure is on that my mind sits on its hands. I was engaged to a girl once, but our nuptial plans were called off because she got tired of being introduced as Miss Uh. Nice girl, too.

I suppose it's due to nervous tension (they say there's a lot of that around these days). It happens every time I act as host. Let me enter a room with a newly arrived couple and I can feel my mental gears grinding together and the transmission locking tight. I stare at the sea of faces, but not a name comes to me. Obviously I knew who everybody was when I invited them here, but now all I can do is murmur lamely, "Well, I guess you probably all know each other already," and beat a hasty retreat to the kitchen.

When it comes to a mental block, I live in the big white house on the corner. Ask me a direct question, and the answer goes and hides under the rug. I know my telephone number perfectly well, but when someone requests it in a hurry I have to look in my address book under "Ford."

Even if I *can* think of a name, it isn't necessarily the right one. This is because I read in some book (the title is right on the tip of my tongue) that you can recollect a person's name by associating it with something it reminds you of. As a result, Mr. Crooker becomes fixed in my mind as Mr. Swindler, Miss Finch is greeted as Miss Birdseed, and Mrs. Burpee turns out to be Mrs. Belch. There's a neighbor in Vermont, a rock-ribbed Republican named Charlie Truman, who has quit speaking to me because I invariably address him as "Harry."

The harder I try to avoid a subject, the more it dominates my conversation. If an acquaintance is sensitive about his balding pate, for example, I'm sure to make some allusion to billiard balls.

Not long ago I was invited to spend the weekend with an old friend at his country place. On our drive out, he confided happily that his wife thought she was pregnant. "Don't say anything about it, though," he added. "The doctor isn't sure yet."

From the moment I arrived, everything I said was loaded. "I'm sorry to barge in on you like this," I told the wife. "You probably weren't expecting a stranger." Feeling my forehead growing warm, I suggested that we take a stroll around the grounds. "You live a long way out of town," I remarked to her. "Do you have any trouble with deliveries?"

Some carpenters were working on a wing to the house, and I observed, "Well, I see you're going to have a new addition shortly." I admired the baby's breath in the garden, I inquired about her shrubs—"Is there a good nursery handy?" Later as we sat on the terrace I commented sentimentally on how nice it was to be together like this in a family way.

This is known as the progressive boo-boo (it gets worse as the consternation grows), and probably the best example is the predicament of a young man I knew whose fiancée brought him home to meet her parents. "Dad's pretty violent about the New Deal," she cautioned, "so don't mention FDR." This weighed on his mind so heavily that when his prospective father-in-law asked how he liked his job, he replied, "Well, to be perfectly franklin ..." His fiancée suggested hurriedly that they might like their coffee in front of the hearth, whereupon the rattled young man assured the father, "I'd certainly enjoy a little fireside chat!" Realizing that her husband was turning purple, the girl's mother tried to change the subject by asking the young man where his home was—at which point he rose abruptly, left the house, and never saw the girl again. "How could I explain that I lived in Roosevelt, Long Island?" he asked me later.

I realized that I am not alone in my cerebral derailments when I read about the banquet chairman whose guest of honor had delivered a lengthy harangue. "Thank you, Professor," he said. "You would have been welcome here tonight if you had said nothing at all." And I cannot help feeling a sympathetic twinge for the Brooklyn lady who asked a visiting author when his personal letters would be published. "Posthumously," he replied. "Oh, I do hope it will be soon!" she gushed.

Which brings to mind a postcard a friend at home sent me while I was traveling abroad recently. "We miss you as much as if you were here," she wrote. I'm still trying to figure that out.

My husband and his sister are notorious yakkers. They can hold court on any subject. One day, he called her. All he had to say was "Hi," and that launched her into a marathon session, going on about this, that, and the other. When she finally paused to come up for air, she had one question: "Who am I talking to?"

— CHRISTINE HOHMAN

Something tells me I need to lose some weight. During a recent trip to visit my son and his family, I stopped off at a bakery to pick up dessert. After scanning the display case, I settled on a dozen pound-cake cupcakes. The clerk's pleasant response: "Is that for here or to go?"

— MIKE COWAN

After my husband injured himself, I ran him over to the doctor's office. There, the nurse dressed his wound and gave him instructions on how to care for it. She then reassured him by adding, "Now, if you do everything I've told you, you won't be with us for long."

— TRUDY MASLOFF

A coworker was telling us all about her recent trip to Las Vegas. "That sounds great. Where did you stay?" asked another colleague.

"I can't remember," she said. "But I think it began with an *S*."

"Was it Caesar's?"

— DARRELL BERGER

On my way to a picnic, I stopped at a fast food place to order a quart of potato salad. "We don't sell it by the quart," the clerk snapped.

"OK, then give me two pints, please," I replied.

I'm proud to say I held my tongue when she asked, "Do you want it in one container?"

— JULIE GUITERREZ

Once, after work, my boss, a self-titled "e-mail man," sent me a text message instructing me to check my e-mail. I rushed over to my computer and pulled up the important missive. It contained two words: "Call me."

— MARTIN HOFFMAN

"Reservations? No, we definitely want to eat here."

"I'll have the fish."

My wife, a professor of medicine, has published five books. After she'd written her latest one, I stopped at a market to buy some chocolate and champagne.

"Are you celebrating something?" asked the clerk as he bagged my items.

"Yes," I replied proudly. "My wife just finished a book." He paused a moment. "Slow reader?"

— DENNIS DOOK

After my speech at a tech conference on "Tips for Going Paperless," I opened the door to questions. "I have one," said a man. "Where are the handouts?"

— MIKE BROWNING

While online looking at used dining room sets with my sister, I mentioned how surprised I was that so many of the tables and chairs were green. "You don't see that color too often in dining rooms," I said. With great patience, she explained, "Mint is the condition, not the color."

— JACKIE GRADY

My niece was thrilled to hear that a new car wash was opening up in her neighborhood.
"How convenient," she said. "I can walk to it."

— CATHY MCCOURT

With the rise of interest in organic foods and "green" living has come a parallel rise in what critics call "greenwashing"— marketing schemes that try to make typical products look more earth-friendly than they actually are.

That's how we ended up with this slogan on the back of a Lay's potato chip bag: "Made with FARM-GROWN potatoes!"

We've made some remarkable advances in agriculture, but there's still no place to grow potatoes besides the dirt. As one wag put it: "At least the potatoes come from a farm, even if the seeds come from a laboratory."

— ANDREW BLECHMAN

After a tourist parked herself on our Washington Island, Wisconsin, trolley, she wanted to know if we had any beaches.

"Yes," I assured her. "Four of them." "Great!" she exclaimed. "Which one's closest to the water?"

— TERRI MOORE

My husband and I are from the "Live Free or Die" state, New Hampshire. Once, while visiting an island in the Caribbean, we started chatting with a resident, and our home state came up.

"I spent the coldest winter of my life in New Hampshire," he told us. "Your state motto really fits— 'Live, Freeze, and Die.' "

— CHRISTINA MCCARTHY

Heading down the interstate, our car passed through a huge swarm of gnats so dense that their bodies made popping noises as they hit the windshield. "I can't get over how loud they are," my wife said.

"Well, we are hitting them at 65 miles per hour," I pointed out.

Her reply left me speechless. "I didn't know bugs could fly that fast."

— JOHN SHINDLEBOWER

Try as I might, I just couldn't get in sync with my insurance customer. When I asked if he lived in the eastern or central time zone, he answered, "We're normal time."

Not sure what that meant, I continued. "Let me put it this way: Is it 10:45 where you are?"

"No," he said. "It's 10:46."

— CHERYL KOCHANEK

Lost in the desert for three days, a man suddenly hears "Mush!"

Looking up, he sees what he thinks is a mirage: a man on a sled, driving a team of huskies. To his surprise, the sled comes to a stop at his feet seconds later.

"I don't know why you're here, but thank goodness," the man says. "I've been lost for days."

Panting, the musher replies, "You think *you're* lost?"

— ROBERT LUTZ

Alice and Ted went snowboarding, and Ted brought along a quart-size thermos.

Alice had never seen one and asked what it was. "It's a thermos," replied Ted. "The guy at the store told me it's used for keeping hot things hot and cold things cold."

"Sounds great," said Alice. "What do you have in it?"

"Three coffees and a Popsicle."

— JEANNE STANTON

One of the guys at the warehouse called my husband, the general manager, to tell him he wouldn't be in that day.

"I'm having my autopsy," he said. "But with any luck I'll be in tomorrow."

— TERRI RITTER

THE WORD GENIUS ISN'T APPLICABLE IN FOOTBALL. A GENIUS IS A GUY LIKE NORMAN EINSTEIN.

— JOE THEISMANN

I'd rather smoke crack than eat cheese from a can.

— GWYNETH PALTROW

I can't really remember the names of the clubs that we went to.

— SHAQUILLE O'NEAL
(Asked if he'd visited the Parthenon while in Greece)

The earth has its boundaries, but human stupidity is infinite.

— GUSTAVE FLAUBERT

I know for a fact it's not in my destiny to die listening to a Britney Spears album, so I always put that on in my [headphones] when I'm flying.

— MEGAN FOX

I think there's a difference between ditzy and dumb. Dumb is just not knowing. Ditzy is having the courage to ask!

— JESSICA SIMPSON

My show is the stupidest show on TV. If you are watching it, get a life.

— JERRY SPRINGER

THE NUMBER OF LINES IN YOUR FOREHEAD TELLS HOW MANY LIVES YOU'VE LIVED.

— ASHTON KUTCHER

A STICKY SITUATION

It was the worst time to
try to save a little money.

By **Marianne Fosnow**

Perhaps I shouldn't have taken my toddler to the grocery store at nap time. Kelly was reaching for everything and trying to climb out of the child seat. In desperation, I reached into my purse and pulled out an orange lollipop. Kelly's face lit up as I unwrapped the treat and handed it to her.

Now I'll be able to concentrate, I thought. I browsed through my coupons, thankful that Kelly was busy and content.

I was so engrossed in finding good deals that I didn't notice the sugary drool dripping down Kelly's chin. It wasn't until she placed a wet, sticky hand on my blouse that I took a good look. The mess was stunning. Almost every inch of her face, her fingertips, and her elbows was sticky. She grinned at me, then stuck out her orange tongue.

Since I was holding at least 40 coupons in my left hand, I dug through my pockets with my right.

I pulled out a small napkin and tried wiping her face. It gave her a paper beard. As I tried to peel it off, she grabbed at the stack of coupons in my other hand and flung them upward. The top and bottom coupon in the stack stuck tight to her hand but every one in between seemed to have been launched into orbit.

Coupons of every size rained down. As soon as they came in contact with my child, they glued fast. Her blue eyes peered over the margarine coupon affixed to her nose. She tried to pull it off, but the paper towel coupon on her hand was in the way. The coupons on each cheek flapped as she cried, "Mama!"

Her alarmed voice seemed to be the only sound in the store. Other shoppers froze in awe, until a few started to giggle. The shopping cart handle looked like a bulletin board.

I had to buy baby wipes to clean her up. The worst part was I knew I had a coupon for them ... somewhere.

AGING
GRACEFULLY

I've been considering a facelift, but it's very expensive, so I've seesawed back and forth. One day my husband and I discussed it yet again, and I asked, "What if I drop dead three months later? Then what would you do?"

After a moment of reflection he offered, "I guess we'd have an open casket."

— CAROL FUGERE

Mother was a health food nut, much to Dad's chagrin. She was always adding wheat germ and other supplements to his food.

"You'll live to be 100 if you keep eating like this," she enthused.

"No, I won't," he muttered as he readied himself for another spoonful of fortified oatmeal. "But it's sure going to seem like it."

— ANNA ZELLER

After my 91-year-old mother finished having her hair cut and shaped, the stylist announced, "There, now you look ten years younger."

My mother, not impressed, replied, "Who wants to look 81 years old?"

— CALVIN UNRUH

When my 85-year-old father was in the hospital, his doctor, trying to determine Dad's mental state, asked,

"What gets you up in the morning?"

My father shrugged. "Probably the same thing as everyone. I have to go to the bathroom."

— MARC ALLEN TROST

No longer relishing my reputation as a technophobe, I bought an iPhone and peppered the young salesman with a ton of questions.

"Please excuse my ignorance," I said. "I'm from the Smith-Corona generation." He had no clue what I was talking about, so I asked, "Do you know what a Smith-Corona is?"

He replied tentatively, "A drink?"

— VICTORIA GEIBEL

I'd noticed that my 60-year-old father seemed to be losing his hearing, so I mentioned it to my mother. "Things haven't changed that much," she said. "The only difference is, before, he didn't listen. Now, he can't."

— DEBORAH KELLY

A group of middle-aged people came into the roller-skating rink my wife and I own. One explained that none of them had skated in 15 years, but they thought it would be fun to give it a try. I had handed out eight pairs of skates before asking the last person in the group what size he needed.

"No thanks," he said. "I'm the designated driver."

— MIKE WILLIAMS

One day, my mother ran into a woman who said they had gone to high school together. Mom insisted she didn't remember her. So the woman came to our house with her yearbook. She pointed out her photo and then my mother's. "Well, of course I didn't recognize you!" Mom said. "You were pretty back then!"

— DEBBIE HAAKENSON

He died doing what he loved: typing his symptoms into WebMD instead of going to the doctor.

— @RISTOLABLE

Two old guys, Fred and Sam, went to the movies. A few minutes into the film, Fred noticed Sam searching for something under his seat.

"What are you doing?" Fred asked.

"Well"—Sam sounded aggravated—"I had a candy in my mouth, but it fell out."

"Forget it. It'll be dirty by now."

"I've got to find it— my teeth are in it."

— FERN HANSEN

My 40-something husband, Jim, was playing basketball with friends his age. "Pretty soon," said one of his teammates, "we'll have to count it as a basket if the ball just hits the rim."

"Yeah," Jim agreed. "It's scary when you have to look through the bottom part of your bifocals to shoot layups and the top part on jump shots."

— PAMELA HELMER

A few years ago, I opened the invitation to my cousin's 100th birthday party. On the front—in bold letters—it screamed, "If he's heard it once, he's heard it a hundred times. Happy Birthday, Sam!"

— LOUIS GLICKMAN

" I don't think I look 30; do you, dear?"

"No, darling, not now. You used to."

— ALABAMA *COURIER*

Midlife Sleep Crisis

On my 40th birthday, I waltzed out of my bedroom dressed in an old outfit.

"I wore this on my 30th birthday. I guess that means my wardrobe is ten years old," I said to my husband, hoping he'd take the hint and buy me some clothes as a present.

"Or," he offered instead, "it means that when you were 30, you had the body of a 40-year-old."

— BETH GEFFERS

We'd finally built our dream home, but the contractor had a concern: the placement of an atrium window for our walk-in shower.

"I'm afraid your neighbors might have a good view of you au naturel," he said.

My middle-aged wife put him at ease. "Don't worry," she said. "They'll only look once."

— GREGG BARNER

Two old friends, Ned and John, lived for baseball. Then one day, John died, leaving Ned inconsolable. A few weeks later, Ned heard someone calling his name. He looked up. Standing on a cloud was his old pal.

"Ned," John called down, "I have good news and bad. The good news is, there's baseball in heaven!"

"Great," said Ned. "What's the bad news?"

"You're pitching Sunday."

— EARL FINCHER

I was having lunch with several 30-something friends when talk turned to the dismal prospect of our growing older.

"Well, judging by my mother," I said, "at least my hearing will improve. My mother can hear my biological clock ticking from 200 miles away."

— SHERRY YATES

My friend was looking at home-gym equipment with her husband. She stepped on a treadmill and said, "Honey, if you buy this for me I will look like I did in high school." "Sweetheart," he said gently, "it's a treadmill, not a time machine."

— LORETTA NISSEN

When a woman I know turned 99 years old, I went to her birthday party and took some photos. A few days later, I brought the whole batch of prints to her so she could choose her favorite.

"Good Lord," she said as she was flipping through them, "I look like I'm 100."

— HELEN B. MARROW

Five years had passed since my last eye exam, and I could tell it was definitely time for another. My vision was getting fuzzier. The eye doctor's receptionist gave me a pre-examination form. One entry was "Reason for visiting the doctor." I couldn't resist. I wrote "Long time no see."

— DAWN ARTESE

After working for months to get in shape, my 42-year-old husband and I hiked to the bottom of the Grand Canyon. At the end of two grueling days, we made it back to the canyon's rim. To celebrate, we each bought an "I hiked the canyon" T-shirt.

About a month later, while my husband was wearing his shirt, a young man approached him. "Did you really hike the canyon?" he asked.

My husband beamed with pride and answered, "Sure did!"

"No kidding!" the fellow said. "What year?"

— CAROL LATKIEWICZ

On my birthday I got a really funny card from a friend. It joked about how our bodies might be getting older, but our minds were still "tarp as shacks."

I wanted to thank the friend who sent the card, but I couldn't.

She forgot to sign it.

— MERIS M. MACK

I was hospitalized with an awful sinus infection that caused the entire left side of my face to swell. On the third day, the nurse led me to believe that I was finally recovering when she announced excitedly, "Look, your wrinkles are coming back!"

— FRANCES M. KRUEGER

At his 103rd birthday party, my grandfather was asked if he thought that he'd be around for his 104th.

"I certainly do," he replied. "Statistics show that very few people die between the ages of 103 and 104."

— HARRY P. COLEMAN

"Not those! At our age, we need all the
preservatives we can get."

Checking out of the grocery store, I noticed the bag boy eyeing my two adopted children. They often draw scrutiny, since my son's a blond Russian while my daughter has shiny black Haitian skin.

The boy continued staring as he carried our groceries to the car. Finally he asked, "Those your kids?"

"They sure are," I said with pride.

"They adopted?"

"Yes," I replied.

"I thought so," he concluded. "I figured you're too old to have kids that small."

— CYNTHIA S. MEYER

I had just had my 50th birthday and found the decade marker traumatic. When I went to get my driver's license renewed, a matter-of-fact woman typed out the information, tested my vision, snapped the camera, and handed me a laminated card with my picture on it.

"You mean I have to look at this for the next four years?" I jokingly said to her.

"Don't worry about it," she replied. "In four years it'll look good to you."

— NANCY FIRESTONE

Paul was in his mid-60s and had just retired. He was planning to landscape his yard and was trying to find some small shrubs or trees.

Burleigh, a 90-year-old from across the street, offered Paul some white-ash saplings that were about two feet tall.

Paul asked, "How long will it take them to be full grown?"

"Twenty years or so," replied Burleigh.

"No good for me, then," said Paul. "I won't be around that long."

The 90-year-old shook his head and replied, "We'll miss ya!"

— CLAUDINE SAVAGE

Timeless Humor from the '80s

■

After the death of her father, my friend tried to persuade her 80-year-old mother to move in with her. The older woman was adamant: "No! Absolutely not! I've always said I'd never live with any of my kids. I've seen too many problems arise from that kind of situation."

My friend said, "Yes, Mom, but you're different."

"I know I am," replied her mother. "But you're not."

— BEA HANSEN

"You can try, but once they're past 40, you
can't teach them new tricks."

FAST TRACK TO A DAD BOD

After nine years, the veteran father explains
how to get the same physique in less time.

By David Tate

DAY 1: Eat a burrito at your steady job during your lunch break.

DAY 2: Have a kid punch you in the groin to wake you up.

DAY 3: Look up how much college tuition will cost, then multiply it by the number of kids you have. Instead of crying, eat a late-night burrito.

DAY 4: Do one push-up, breathe heavily, and then open a bag of Wild Berry Skittles.

DAY 5: Buy a gym membership. When they give you a tour, take a good look around—this is the last time you will see it all.

DAY 6: Look at yourself in the mirror while recalling that how you look has nothing to do with your chances of getting lucky today and that this is true every day forever after.

DAY 7: Carry a child for an entire zoo trip in your left arm, even after you can no longer feel it.

DAY 8: Get four hours of sleep, allow your body to confuse being tired with hunger, and eat two burritos.

DAY 9: Chase a balloon across the parking lot of a Toys"R"Us at a "death struggle" level of intensity. Return it to the birthday girl, and wait until she smiles at you and says, "Thank you, Daddy," before you throw up in the bushes.

DAY 10: Remember that time you were good at sports? Man, wasn't that so great?

DAY 11: Start running but immediately injure your entire body, and then take a year off.

DAY 12: Lower your testosterone level a bit by losing yet another negotiation with a two-year-old.

DAY 13: Reward yourself with a milkshake for waking up today.

DAY 14: Play basketball with the grade-school kids in your neighborhood. Spend the time in the hospital catching up on your sleep.

DAY 15: Let the stress of your current financial burden allow you to feel each individual hair turning white.

DAY 16: Take your blood pressure pill, but only after stressing about having to take a blood pressure pill.

DAY 17: Eat some Oven Baked Cheetos. If you don't have any on hand, get married, and they will appear where your regular Cheetos used to be.

DAY 18: Squat down to wipe up vomit; raise up with your back.

DAY 19: Whenever you see a pull-up bar, grab it and pretend you are about to knock out some pull-ups. Wonder quietly what doing a single pull-up feels like.

DAY 20: Go to the pool and confidently take off your shirt and swim a couple of laps. Put your shirt back on and quietly dry-heave in the car.

DAY 21: Show off your new dad bod to your wife by first flagging her down on Facebook. Ignore her eye roll and laughter—she isn't in touch with how attracted to you she is right now.

When I checked into a motel, I noticed a card in our room indicating that guests 55 or older received a seniors' discount. As a newly minted 55-year-old, I returned to the front desk armed with my photo ID. Imagine my chagrin when the clerk told me he had already given me the discount!

— JACKIE GREENHALGH

After church one Sunday, my wife, Norma, and I went out for lunch. Outside the restaurant, a schoolmate I hadn't seen for 50 years recognized me, and we stopped to chat while my wife went ahead into the restaurant.

"Wow!" I said when I joined Norma inside, "That guy told me I haven't changed since Grade 9."

Norma laughed. "You mean," she said, "you looked that old when you were in Grade 9?"

— WOLF MAYDELL

more questions."

"Why?" she asked.

"Because all of those answers were on his badge."

— WEBB SMITH

My 85-year-old grandfather was rushed to the hospital with a possible concussion. The doctor asked him a series of questions:

"Do you know where you are?"

"The hospital."

"What city are you in?"

"Raleigh."

"Do you know who I am?"

"Dr. Hamilton."

My grandfather then turned to the nurse and said, "I hope he doesn't ask me any

Timeless Humor from the 2000s

■

"I think my wife's going deaf," Joe told their doctor.

"Try to test her hearing at home and let me know how severe her problem is before you bring her in for treatment," the doctor said.

So that evening, when his wife was preparing dinner, Joe stood 15 feet behind her and said, "What's for dinner, honey?" No response. He moved to ten feet behind her and asked again. No response. Then he stood five feet in back of her and tried again but still got no answer.

Finally, he stood directly behind her and asked, "Honey, what's for supper?"

She turned around. "For the fourth time—I said chicken!"

— GORDON BAYLIS

My college roommate and I have remained good friends, and now that we're hitting middle age, I never miss a chance to kid him about being older than I am—even if it's only by one month. So for his 40th birthday I gave him a not-so-subtle jab by gift-wrapping a CD by the British reggae group UB40.

A month later, he sent me my own birthday gift—the latest release from the Irish rock band U2.

— JOHN DAVIS

When my husband returned from a jog, I joked, "What are you running from?"

"Old age," he said.

"Oh yeah? Then what are those gray hairs on your head?"

"Camouflage."

— ANN HANSEN

An old man was rowing a boat on a lake when a frog swam up to him and yelled, "Mister! Mister! I'm really a beautiful princess. Kiss me and we'll live happily ever after!" The man put the frog in his pocket and rowed to shore. The frog called out again, "Hey, mister! I'm really a gorgeous princess. Kiss me and we'll live happily ever after."

Still the man said nothing and walked down the road toward town. The frog was getting angry at being ignored. "Why don't you kiss me? I told you I'm really a beautiful princess."

"Listen, lady," the man replied. "I'm 90 years old. At this point in my life I'd rather have a talking frog."

— CHANTELL WILLIAMS

Our group was third in line behind two other foursomes at the golf course. A young man in the first group walloped his tee shot straight down the middle of the 410-yard fairway to within a few yards of the green.

"Wow," said an older man in the second foursome, "I don't even go that far on vacation."

— RICHARD C. PETERS

I'm not keen on taking pills, so when my doctor gave me a prescription to lower my blood pressure, I asked him if there were any side effects. "Yes," he said. "Longevity."

— BELLA KELLY

During a visit with a friend at an assisted living center, I was invited to stay for lunch. As we entered the cafeteria, she leaned toward me and whispered, "They have two lines here. We call them cane and able."

— MARTHA LEONARD

Our family was at an outdoor fair watching a caricature artist at work when a 50-something woman stopped to watch as well. When she saw that the artist charged $15 for a color caricature, she gasped, "Fifteen dollars—just to have someone draw my wrinkles!"

The artist turned slowly and studied her face for a moment before replying, "I don't see any wrinkles."

She immediately sat down and had her portrait drawn.

— MARGARET WELLS

You come from dust. You will return to dust. That is why I don't dust.

It could be someone I know.

— NICK GIDWANI

Shortly after my father's death, my 90-year-old grandmother insisted that my mother have a complete physical. After some debate, my mother reluctantly made an appointment. The doctor not only gave her a clean bill of health but remarked that she'd probably live to be 110.

To our surprise, my grandmother did not seem entirely pleased by the good report. She sat quietly for a few minutes, then said with a sigh, "And just what am I going to do with a 110-year-old daughter?"

— B.L.M.

The cardiologist at the ER had bad news for me: "You're going to need a pacemaker."

Later, the nurse filling out the admission form began to ask me the standard questions: "Have you ever had mumps, measles, etc.?"

Seeing how upset I was, she put down the clipboard and took my hand. "Don't worry," she said soothingly. "This kind of heart problem is easily fixed, and your life will be much better as a result."

I felt reassured until she continued: "Do you have a living will?"

— ROBERT PORTER

You are only young once. After that you have to think up some other excuse.

— BILLY ARTHUR

Feeling down about my thinning hair, I told a friend, "Soon I'll never need to go back to the beauty salon. Whenever I vacuum, all I pick up is my hair."

A glass-half-full kind of gal, she responded, "Well, then you won't need to vacuum either."

— AGNES SCHARENBROCH

I heard an older woman complain about her aches. But her friend one-upped her: "I woke up this morning and thought I was dead because nothing hurt."

— NANCY KUNKEL

Though I often pride myself on appearing younger than my 59 years, I had a reality check when I brought my mother back to the nursing home after a visit with us. As I struggled with her suitcases, two elderly gentlemen held the door open for me.

"We hope you will be very happy here," one of them said to me.

— MARION CLOUSE

When the new activities director for the rec center walked in, all of us retirees quickly took notice. She was 20-something, statuesque, and gorgeous. My buddy whispered, "She makes me wish I was 30 years older."

"Don't you mean 30 years younger?" I asked.

"No. If I were 30 years younger, I'd still never have a chance with a woman like that. If I were 30 years older, it wouldn't bother me so much."

— JOHN BERTSCHLER

The woman in front of me at the motor vehicles office was taking the eye test, first with her glasses on, then off. "Here's your license," the examiner said when she was done. "But there's a restriction. You need to wear glasses to drive your car."

"Honey," the woman declared. "I need my glasses to find my car."

— NICOLE HAAKE

Sad after the funeral of a friend, my wife and I ducked into a Chinese restaurant for a little Szechuan pick-me-up. The feel-good session ended abruptly when I read the fortune in my cookie: "You will soon be reunited with a good friend."

— STANLEY HEERBOTH

ANYONE OF MY AGE KNOWS THAT DAYS PASS AT A FAR GREATER SPEED THAN WHEN THEY WERE YOUNG.

— PRINCE CHARLES

I don't understand why people say "I don't want to live forever." Why not?

— ALAN ALDA

I keep getting asked, "What's the secret of your longevity?" I say, "I haven't died."

— BILLY JOEL

You know you're getting old when you get that one candle on the cake. It's like, "See if you can blow this out."

— JERRY SEINFELD

You can't get hung up on age or beauty, because then you're always chasing after something you'll never get back.

— TINA TURNER

My mother always used to say, "The older you get, the better you get. Unless you're a banana."

— BETTY WHITE

Who wants to reach the end of their life in a perfectly preserved body? The scars and the crinkles and the cracks are what make us interesting.

— BEAR GRYLLS

NOTHING LOOKS BETTER IN YOUR 50s THAN SUNSCREEN IN YOUR 20s.

— JENNIFER GARNER

THE QUEEN OF SPIN

Aunt Lucy was a hot ticket.

By **June Czarnezki**

My sister **Mona** and I loved to ice-skate on a pond near our house in the 1970s. We were teenagers and enjoyed pretending to be Olympic gold medalist Dorothy Hamill.

In my family, skates were an extra, something I needed to earn money to buy for myself. I'd found a pair of black ones at a rummage sale. Only boys wore black skates, but they were all I could afford. Mona acted smug about the white skates she'd borrowed.

Our Aunt Lucy lived nearby and sometimes met us at the pond. We figured that, at 36, she was much too old to skate. When I brought out the black skates, she noticed how I frowned putting them on. She asked me if I wanted to wear hers.

I looked at them. They were the right size, but they were fire-engine red. My black skates were bad enough—red ones were out of the question.

"No way," I said. So Aunt Lucy laced up her red skates, stepped onto the ice, and began to skate.

Mona and I gaped: In the middle of the pond, Aunt Lucy pirouetted like the ballerina in my jewelry box. With all eyes on her, she skated backward, spun, and jumped. Some kids started laughing at her, pointing at the red skates, but Aunt Lucy just smiled and continued to twirl. Embarrassed at the spectacle of our skating relative, Mona and I kept our distance.

The kids continued their behavior until Aunt Lucy skated up to them. She said something we couldn't hear, but then they stopped laughing. Their expressions changed to awe. Back in the warming shack, we asked Aunt Lucy what she'd said. "I told them that I was a professional skater for Holiday on Ice," she said, "And that I wore the red skates in last night's performance."

We all had a good laugh at Aunt Lucy's made-up story. And we learned that red skates and a little white lie can make you a star.

MODERN LOVE

Although I'd been dating a woman for several months, I guess I didn't know her as well as I thought. One day I called, and her ten-year-old son answered.

"Hi," I said. "It's Tom. Can I speak with your mom?"

He responded, "Are you Tom One or Tom Two?"

Needless to say, his mother is now down to one Tom.

— THOMAS FALLDORF

I had to voice my concern when a coworker said she found dates using the Internet.

"Don't worry about me," she said. "I always insist we meet at a miniature golf course."

"Why there?" I asked.

"First, it's a public spot," she said. "Second, it's in broad daylight. And third, I have a club in my hand."

— LINDA AKINS

When we finished a personality assessment at work, I asked my friend Dan if he would share the results with his wife. "That would require me to go home and say, 'Hi, honey. I just paid someone $400 to tell me what's wrong with me,'" he said. "And based on that, considering we've been married 23 years, she'd hand me a bill for $798,000."

— RON JAMES

My teenage son and I were discussing dating and relationships. To impress upon him that I had valuable experience to share, I commented, "You know, I've been around the barn a few times."

"Yeah, Mom," he said, unimpressed, "but always on the same horse."

— NANCY WEST

Timeless Humor from the '50s

■

Recuperating from an operation, I began to wonder if the young doctor who was looking after me was competent. He always had such a dreamy, faraway look in his eyes. But when the day came for him to remove my stitches, he attacked the job with unusual concentration. And, as each stitch came out, he whispered something under his breath. When he got to the last one, he held it up and beamed at me. "She loves me!" he confided gleefully.

— G. F. KRUPP

As a single, never-married woman in my 40s, I have been questioned endlessly about my status by friends, relatives and coworkers. Over the years I've noticed a subtle change in the nature of their inquiries.

In my teens, friends would ask, "Who are you going out with this weekend?"

In my 20s, relatives would say, "Who are you dating?"

In my 30s, coworkers might inquire, "So, are you dating anyone?"

Now people ask, "Where did you get that adorable purse?

— **MARY A. ELDER**

A woman friend looked at my chest and said, "Of course." That's when I realized I was wearing a T-shirt I had picked up at the annual biker rally in Sturgis, South Dakota. It read "If a

I felt like my boyfriend, Brian, was taking me for granted. "You're never home," I complained. "All you want to do is hang out with your buddies. We only go out if they're not available."

"That's not true," Brian protested. "You know I'd rather be with you than have fun."

— **LISA SIMONS**

man says something in the woods where no woman can hear, is he still wrong?"

— **RUSS HARGREAVES**

A man came through my lane at the grocery store with a jug of wine and a bouquet of roses. But before paying, he set the two items aside and said, "I'll be right back." He ran off, only to return a minute later with a second jug of wine and another bouquet of roses.

"Two girlfriends?" I asked.

"No," he said. "Just one really angry one."

— **JOHN H. FLYNN**

I'll never find the right guy," I heard the young guest at the wedding shower sigh.

"Don't give up," urged an older woman. "Every pot has a lid."

"Or," a cynical voice behind her offered, "you could just be a skillet."

— **GEORGIANNA GUTHRIE**

My boyfriend Hans and I met online. After dating a long time, I introduced him to my uncle, who was fascinated by the fact that we met over the Internet. He asked Hans what kind of line he had used to pick me up. Ever the geek, Hans naively replied, "I just used a modem."

— **ANNE MCCONNELL**

"I can handle my wife's Honey-Do list. It's her Honey-Don't list that just about kills me."

An enormously wealthy 65-year-old man falls in love with a young woman in her 20s and is contemplating a proposal. "Do you think she'd marry me if I tell her I'm 45?" he asks his friend.

"Your chances are better," says the friend, "if you tell her you're 90."

— PROSANTA CHAKRABARTY

My friend Tim took Mary out for a romantic dinner where conversation turned toward marriage. Tim had been saving for an engagement ring, but he was in graduate school and in dire need of a computer. Mary was understanding, telling Tim they had the rest of their lives to get engaged, so he should use his savings to buy a computer instead.

During dessert, Tim suddenly reached into his pocket and pulled out an engagement ring. Mary was stunned. But after she collected herself, she looked up and prompted, "Well, don't you have something to ask me?"

Tim then got down on bended knee. "Honey," he said, "will you buy me a computer?"

— CHRISTINE LAUBE

It was my wedding day, and no one was happier than my 78-year-old mother. But as she approached the church doors, an usher asked, "Which side are you on?"

"Oh, no," she said. "Are they fighting already?"

— JOSEPH HUBISZ

When I told my parents that I was getting married, my excited mother said, "You have to have the rehearsal dinner someplace opulent, where there's dancing."

My father, seeing where this was heading, said, "I'll pay you $1,000 to elope."

"And you have to have a breakfast, for the people who are coming from out of town."

"Two thousand."

"We'll need a photographer. Oh, and what colors do you want for the reception?"

"Five thousand!"

We eloped to Spain.

— MARY NICHOLS

My granddaughter asked why I called my husband Hon. "It's a term of endearment," I explained.

My husband mumbled, "After more than 40 years, it's a term of endurement."

— MARILYN KLATT

Before going out to a movie, my husband and I stopped at the town dump to drop off some garbage. As I waited for him in our pickup truck, a man walked by. Glancing at my dress and jewelry, he said, "I certainly hope this isn't your first date."

— VIDA MCHOES PICKETT

Asked my husband to bring me a cookie. He brought me the whole box. We're soul mates.

— @WINOSAURUSMOM

Driving home from our friend's house, my husband and I passed a garage where a father and son were working together on a car. Warm feelings flooded through me as I noticed my husband's smile. I was thinking about starting a family and was happy that he exhibited the same desire until he mused, "I sure wish we had a garage."

— KIMBERLY PRAY

My husband's expanding waistline was a sore subject, but I could no longer ignore it, especially since he's still young and handsome.

"Honey," I said, using my seductive voice, "if you lose 20 pounds, I promise to dance for you."

Using his sarcastic voice, he shot back, "Lose 10 pounds, and I'll watch."

— EMILY GURLEY

Surfing the Net, I came across a movie poster of a man and woman kissing passionately in the pouring rain. I called my husband over. "How come you never kiss me like that?"

He studied the sodden couple. "Because we haven't had that much rain."

— SERENA S.

Friend #1: Are you visiting us tomorrow? Do you need directions?

Friend #2: I'm all set. I have the address, a GPS, and a GPS override.

Friend #1: What's a GPS override?

Friend #2: My wife.

— BALASUBRAMANIAN VENKATARAMAN

If the power goes out across North America, don't panic. My wife has enough candles stored away for everyone.

— @SQUIRREL4WKGN

"You keep giving me advice when what
I need is herbal tea and lemon bars."

One morning I found a beautiful long-stemmed rose lying by the kitchen sink. Even though the flower was plastic, I was thinking how, after all the years we had been married, my husband could still make such a wonderful romantic gesture. Then I noticed a love note lying next to it. "Dear Sue," it read. "Don't touch the rose. I'm using the stem to unclog the drain."

— SUZAN L. WIENER

Clearly, my husband and I need to brush up on our flirting. The other night, after I crawled into bed next to him, he wrapped his large arms around me, drew a deep breath, and whispered, "Mmm ... that Vicks smells good."

— REBECCA RIZZUTI

My wife asked me if I thought she looked fat in her new dress. Pointing to what I was wearing, I replied, "Do I look stupid in this shirt?"

— BRIAN RICE

My husband, Mike, and I had several stressful months of financial difficulties. So one evening I was touched to see him gazing at the diamond wedding ring that symbolized our marriage.

"With this ring ..." I began romantically.

"We could pay off Visa," he responded.

— DAWN HILL

For a romantic touch, I washed our sheets with lavender-scented detergent. When my husband got into bed, he sniffed. "What's this?" he asked.

"Guess," I said coyly.

"I have no idea," he said. "It smells like the stuff you use to line the hamster's cage."

— KATHLEEN WATERS

Timeless Humor from the '80s

■

Ada told us how she watched her newly retired husband rearrange the contents of all her kitchen shelves.

"Didn't you try to stop him?" one of her friends asked. "Didn't you say something to him?"

"No," Ada said calmly. "I just waited until he was through. Then I went down to the basement and rearranged his tools."

— DOROTHY BRAZIER

"Romance has nothing to do with it. Dan and I are renewing our marriage vows because he's forgotten them."

65 MILLION WOMEN WANT MY HUSBAND

When America's zaniest middle-aged housewife tries to put some romance back in her marriage, the result is about as exciting as a bride with a lip full of Novocain.

By Erma Bombeck

All the way to Jill's cocktail party, I had a feeling of exhilaration. For the first time in a long time, my life was coming together. I no longer anguished over what I looked like. I had come to grips with domesticity. All three kids were not only speaking to us, but our 24-year-old daughter even openly displayed a curiosity as to how to turn on the stove.

The pressures of child raising were easing off. I stopped eating chocolates in the closet and dedicating my life to putting toilet seats down. In my awkward way, I was re-entering the human race after 20 years of Edith-Bunkering it.

My eyes danced as we entered the room. I spotted my old friend Phyllis. I hadn't seen her in ages.

"Phyllis!" I shouted. "How long has it been? Do you still bowl with the league on Tuesdays?"

Phyllis set down her glass without smiling. "Bowl? That was only a transference of aggression to keep me from dealing with my realities head-on."

"C'mon," I laughed.

"You remember how I used to have anxiety attacks when I emptied the sweeper bag? Well, the bottom line was I was in a crisis situation I couldn't handle. So, I began to read self-help books to raise my consciousness level. Right now, I'm reading *Sensual Needlepoint* by Candy Summers."

"*Sensual Needlepoint*?" I said, gulping my drink. "What's happened to you? You used to be so shallow!"

She ignored my comment. "Do you know what s wrong with you?" she asked, leaning closer. "Sex! You're not in touch with your feelings. You and your husband are probably just plain bored with one another. It happens in a lot of marriages."

"Phyllis, *you're* the one who was too shy to tell anyone you were pregnant. You told everyone you had 'something in the oven.' You raised children who thought it took nine months to bake a pie!"

"Well, things are different now," said Phyllis. "I know that sex is something you have to work on in a marriage. You need Marybelle Morganstein."

"You mean the author of *The Sub-Total Woman*? I've heard of her."

"Heard of her!" shouted Phyllis. "Are you serious? I tell you what. I'll loan you my copy."

"I do not need help from *The Sub-Total Woman*."

"When was the last time you bathed with your husband?"

"When we washed the dog."

Phyllis was wacko—no doubt about it. I eased away and observed my husband across the room. For a man going through his metallic age (silver hair, gold teeth, lead bottom), he did cut quite a figure.

I reflected: Marybelle Morganstein had been on all the talk shows touting her book and saying things like "When a man's got cream in the refrigerator at home, he won't go out looking for 2 percent butterfat."

She had appeared on a sex-themed TV show and talked about the Compatible Quiz. At first, it bothered me to know that, without taking it, I'd probably flunk it. And after 30 years of marriage and three children, I didn't want to know that my husband and I were incompatible. But I couldn't resist. It went like this:

You and your husband are alone in a cabin for the first time since your marriage. He is nibbling on your ear. Do you (a) nibble back or (b) tell him the toilet is running?

Your husband comes home unexpectedly in the middle of the afternoon. Do you (a) slip into something suggestive and make him an offer he can't refuse or (b) leave him there and go to a food-processor demonstration?

Your husband invites you to go to a convention where you will share only your evenings together. Do you (a) get a babysitter and go or (b) regard it as a great time to stay at home and paint the bedroom?

I didn't have to go on. The results were obvious. I had become a woman who didn't pamper her husband and didn't serve his needs. Maybe Phyllis was right. Maybe we *had* fallen into a rut. We weren't demonstrative people—I'd feel like a fool paddling around after him. On the other hand, what if someday he developed a craving for 2 percent butterfat? If Marybelle Morganstein called her husband at the office every day just to pant into his ear over the phone, maybe it was worth it.

The next morning my husband called from the bathroom: "What's this?"

On the mirror, in lipstick, I had written: 65 MILLION WOMEN WANT MY HUSBAND!

"It's just a reminder, dear, how lucky I am to have you."

He studied the mirror carefully and said, "Name names."

"Don't get testy. Marybelle Morganstein says that if women treated their husbands better, they wouldn't wander."

"Who is Marybelle Morganstein, and where am I going?"

"She's going to put some spark in our marriage. Here is your shaver, your bath towel, your soap, and your shampoo."

"Where's my rubber duck?" he asked irritably.

"And your comb, your deodorant, your clean shirt, and your trousers. Let me put that lid down for you."

"GET OUT OF THE BATHROOM!" he yelled through clenched teeth.

When he was gone, I went back to *The Sub-Total Woman* for reassurance. It appeared on page 110. "In a survey of 10,000 males," it read, "almost half of them said they cheated on their wives and most

> ## For a man in his metallic phase (silver hair, gold teeth), he cut quite a figure.

said they wanted or needed some physical display of affection."

Just after lunch, I went to the phone and called my husband. "Hello," I said, trying to make my voice sound throaty. "Could you come home early?"

"Whatsa matter?" he asked. "Do you have a dental appointment?"

"Come home early and you can have your way with me."

"Hang on a second. Another call is coming through," he said.

I hung up the phone and went back to Marybelle's book. "Jar your husband out of his lethargy by meeting him at the door dressed in something outrageous—like a cheerleader, a bunny, or a slave girl."

A costume. Was she serious?

Even at Halloween, I just put brown grocery bags over the kids' heads, cut eyes in them, and told them to tell everyone their mother was having surgery. I wasn't good at costumes. But I went through all the closets. The only thing I could come up with was a pair of my son's football pants, a jersey, and a helmet. I felt about as sensuous as a bride with a lip full of Novocain.

When I heard the car in the driveway, I flung open the front door and yelled, "It's a scoreless game so far!"

The washer repairman didn't say anything for a couple of minutes. His eyes never met mine. He just stared at the floor and mumbled, "It says here on the work sheet that your dryer won't heat up." I cleared my throat. "Right, come in. The dryer is next to the washer behind the louvered doors." Neither of us spoke. The only sound was of my cleats clicking on the tile. He worked in silence and I disappeared to the other end of the house.

I got out of the football uniform and into a dress. I wasn't ready for the Sub-Total Super Bowl, and I knew it. When my husband got home, we ate dinner between *The Liar's Club* and *Name That Tune*. The kids fanned in and out like a revolving door. There were clothes to fold, purchases to discuss, decisions to be made. I never realized what a holding pattern we were in until I tried to massage my husband's neck and he said, "I'll save you time. My billfold's on the dresser."

I returned to folding clothes. About 11 p.m., we both heard the smoke alarm go off in our bedroom and rushed back to see my sheer red nightgown smoking from the heat of a lightbulb.

"Why is your nightgown draped over the lamp?" asked my husband evenly.

"I am creating a mood."

"For a disaster movie?"

"It was supposed to give the room a sexy, sensuous feeling."

"Open the window. If it gets any sexier in here, I'm going to pass out."

It was an hour before the smoke cleared and we could go to bed.

"Did you call me today or did I imagine it?" he asked.

"I called."

"What did you want?"

"I wanted to tell you to come home early and you could have your way with me."

"You should have left a message," he yawned, and crawled into bed.

I turned on the bathroom light. The mirror still reflected: 65 MILLION WOMEN WANT MY HUSBAND!

I took out a deodorant stick and wrote under it: WHY?

During a consultation with her doctor before having surgery, my friend said to him, "My husband wants me to ask when I will be able to—"

The doctor cut her off right there. "I'm asked that question frequently," he said. He then leaned in and added, "You need to wait at least six weeks for intimacy."

My friend shook her head. "No, what he wanted to know was when I will be able to cook for him."

— MICHELLE HOSKINS

Both of my parents work and lead hectic lives. So my father was bound to forget their wedding anniversary.

Remembering at the last minute, he sped to the stationery store, flew through the door, and breathlessly asked the sales clerk, "Where are the anniversary cards?"

To his surprise he heard my mother call out, "Over here, Bill."

— ELIZABETH RANSOM

"Perhaps you've heard of me. I discovered a little thing called fire."

After my husband and I had a huge argument, we ended up not talking to each other for days. Finally, on the third day, he asked where one of his shirts was. "Oh," I said, "now you're speaking to me."

He looked confused. "What are you talking about?"

"Haven't you noticed I haven't spoken to you for three days?" I challenged.

"No," he said. "I just thought we were getting along."

— BETH DORIA

My husband and I, married 13 years, were dressing for a party. I'd spent all day getting a haircut and permanent, then as we were leaving, we met in the hall and he said nothing. I complained that he had not even noticed my hair. "You used to pay attention to every little thing, and now you don't

At a Hollywood wedding reception, one woman remarked how lovely the star looked as a bride, and another said sweetly, "Oh, she always does. She's thrown a bridal bouquet often enough to have pitched a nine-inning game."

— EDDIE CANTOR

notice anything! You take me for granted!"

My husband stood there rubbing his face as he let me rant and rave. Then it hit me: He'd shaved off his six-month-old beard.

— MELONY ANDERSON

A man is drinking with his wife when out of the blue he says, "I love you."

"Is that you or your beer talking?" she asks.

"It's me," he says, "talking to the beer."

— PLANET PROCTOR

My cell phone quit as I tried to let my wife know that I was caught in freeway gridlock and would be late for our

anniversary dinner. I wrote a message on my laptop asking other motorists to call her, printed it on a portable inkjet and taped it to my rear windshield.

When I finally arrived home, my wife gave me the longest kiss ever. "I really think you love me," she said. "At least 70 people called and told me so."

— JARON SUMMERS

My parents divorced when I was two but remained friends. So much so that on my wedding day, Dad toasted my husband and me by saying, "I hope y'all are as happy together as your mother and I are apart."

— MELANIE FRANKLIN

"You've done something different with your hair."

When a friend's marriage began to unravel, my 12-year-old son offered, "I think the problem is largely psychological."

"How so?" I asked.

"He's psycho and she's logical."

— DEBORAH MOLER

My ex-husband was both difficult and prescient. Before our wedding, I declared in a fit of pique, "John, I don't know if I should marry you or leave you."

John replied, "Well, baby, you'll probably do both."

— JANET STREET

Considering divorce, I was feeling pretty blue. "It's not just me," I whined to my mother. "Do you know anyone who is happily married?"

Mom nodded. "Your father."

—C. HEINECK

As the music swelled during a recent wedding reception, my hopelessly romantic husband squeezed my hand, leaned in, and said, "You are better looking than half the women here."

— MARLENE BAMBRICK

Purely by coincidence, I ran into my husband in our local grocery store on Valentine's Day. Tom was carrying a beautiful pink azalea, and I joked, "That better be for me."

From behind, a woman's voice: "It is now."

— PATRICIA RUT

My wife and I were going through a rough patch financially, but we kept ourselves sane by repeating, "As long as we have each other, we don't need anything else." But when the television and radio in our bedroom broke within a few days of each other, my wife lost it.

"That's just great!" she shouted. "Now there's no entertainment in our bedroom at all!"

— VINCENT DAY

A guy tells his friend, "I bought my wife a diamond ring."

"You told me she wanted a car," the friend replies.

"Yeah," says the first guy, "but where would I find a fake car?"

— S.L.

Recently engaged, my brother-in-law Jeff brought his fiancée home to meet the family. When asked if she was enjoying herself, she politely replied yes. "She would say that," Jeff interjected. "She's not the type to say no."

"I see," my husband said after a brief silence. "And that explains the engagement."

— ALLISON BEVANS

While working for the Social Security Administration, I helped an elderly woman—who was no longer married—fill out her claim form.

Reading off a question, I asked, "How did your marriage end?"

"Just fine," she said, grinning a little too broadly. "He died."

— WILLIS BIRD

When my wife gets a little upset, sometimes a simple "Calm down" in a soothing voice is all it takes to get her a lot upset.

— @THENARDVARK (BRYAN DONALDSON)

ALL YOU NEED IS LOVE. BUT A LITTLE CHOCOLATE NOW AND THEN DOESN'T HURT.

— CHARLES M. SCHULZ

A couple that golfs together stays together. Where else can I walk six miles and talk to my husband for four hours without distraction?

— NORAH O'DONNELL

In all the chaos going on, we need a little love and romance.

— DIANA KRALL

It's not what you've accomplished, it's the relationships you have. You're survived by things that matter— the people you love and those who love you back.

— CHRIS EVANS

Behind every great man is a woman rolling her eyes.

— JIM CARREY
in *Bruce Almighty*

The formula for a happy marriage? It's the same as the one for living in California: When you find a fault, don't dwell on it.

— JAY TRACHMAN

Love is like an endless cup of coffee at a crappy diner, only it won't give you heartburn and you'll actually enjoy it.

— NORA MCINERNY

ALL I NEED IN A RELATIONSHIP IS SOMEONE TO WATCH TV WITH ME.

— JENNIFER LAWRENCE

WARDROBE DECISION LEAVES HER IN A BIND

The skinny: Svelte comes at a price.

By Rosemary Williams

When I was 17, Bill, a handsome Yale senior, asked me to go with him and another couple to see the circus in New York. I wanted to look chic, gorgeous, and slim—and the fastest way to achieve this in the 1950s was with a girdle.

When he picked me up, he said, "You look very pretty." Success, I thought. Even if the girdle pinches.

During the long subway ride into Manhattan, I was uncomfortable. By the time we got to Madison Square Garden, I fervently wished I hadn't worn the thing. Metal stays cut into my sides, back, and belly, causing constant pain I tried to ignore.

We entered at the sideshow, where we talked to the fat lady, and watched a sword swallower and jugglers. Then we bought some peanuts to feed to the elephants. We climbed up, up, up to our seats at the very top of the arena. From this vantage point we could look directly into the eyes of the tightrope walkers.

Midway through the show I could no longer stand it. I whispered to Bill, "Please excuse me, I'll be right back." I stepped over what seemed like hundreds of knees, down, down, down to the ladies' room. I rushed into a cubicle and pulled off the girdle.

What now? I had my umbrella with me so I stuffed it in there. Then I took a deep breath, and my body relaxed.

Back I went up to my seat and finally began to enjoy myself. It was a great night.

Leaving the Garden, Bill offered to carry my umbrella, and as we stepped outside, it was raining. Before I could stop him, he opened the umbrella—and the girdle plopped right into a puddle. For a moment we all stared at it. Then the three of them howled with laughter.

Realizing I had to do something, I grabbed the girdle and dropped it into a nearby garbage pail. Soon I was giggling too.

HUMOR
IN
UNIFORM

On his first day of Army basic training,
my husband stood with the other recruits as the
sergeant asked, "How many of you are smokers?"
Several men raised their hands.
"Congratulations!" he said. "You just quit."

— CHRISTINA KOSATKA

During reservists' training, my commanding officer was briefing his colleagues on the battalion's mission. While he was highlighting the key objectives of our task—serious business, aimed at motivating the troops—he was suddenly interrupted by a ringing cell phone. The tune? The *Mission: Impossible* theme.

— SAMUEL HENRY

When my husband visited our son, Michael, at boot camp, he found him marching smartly with his unit. He proudly approached the soldiers and began to snap photo after photo. Embarrassed and worried about getting into trouble, Michael looked straight ahead and didn't change his expression.

Suddenly his drill sergeant barked, "Comito, give me 25 push-ups. And the next time your daddy wants your picture, you smile!"

— EDYTHE COMITO

It was our first day on the rifle range at Lackland Air Force Base. I felt confident as I aimed and squeezed the trigger of my carbine for my first shot. "Good news and bad news," my instructor said. "The good news: You got a bull's-eye." Before my head could swell too much, he added, "But it was in somebody else's target."

— GENE NEWMAN

Following a few frantic minutes, air traffic controllers finally made radio contact with the lost young pilot. "What was your last known position?" they asked.

"When I was No. 1 for takeoff," came the reply.

— PHYLLIS NIELSON

It was basic training, and I was seated in the barber chair bemoaning the impending loss of my hair when the barber asked, "Where are you from?"

"St. Louis," I grumbled.

"Hey, I'm from St. Louis too!" he said. He then asked conspiratorially, "Do you want to keep your sideburns?"

I perked up. "Sure!"

With that, he revved up the razor, clipped off my sideburns, and gave them to me. As I left the barbershop with sideburns in hand, I heard him ask his next victim, "Where are you from?"

"Chicago."

"Hey, I'm from Chicago too!"

— STEVE FINKELSTEIN

When I was a Navy student pilot, I visited the home of a classmate. I met his wife and baby and was impressed that he had all his flight gear neatly laid out on a table. But something struck me as odd.

Picking up some unidentifiable gear, I said, "I didn't get one of these!"

"Um, no, you're good," he mumbled. "That's my wife's breast pump."

— CURT GREGORY

Timeless Humor from the '50s

■

A young soldier, just out of basic training, came into my office at Camp Gordon, Georgia, a few days before Christmas. Orders had been issued permitting half of the camp to go home for Christmas and the other half for New Year's. This soldier's name was on the New Year's list and he wanted it switched to the Christmas list. When I asked him why, he said that he wanted to go home with his mother for Christmas. I reminded him that 20,000 other men in our camp wanted to do the same.

"No, chaplain," he replied, "I'm the only one who wants to go *with* his mother. You see, my mother is a WAC and her sergeant is letting her go home for Christmas."

— REV. RAYMOND G. HEISEL

A sergeant was trying to sell us new soldiers on the idea of joining the airborne division. His pitch clearly needed work. "The first week, we separate the men from the boys," he began. "The second week, we separate the men from the idiots. The third week, the idiots jump."

— JIMMY RONEY

*"Not bad, kid, but you'd be vulnerable
to attacks here and here."*

A **senior in** the high school class I taught was always in trouble, both at home and at school, and he was getting fed up. "That's it! I'm tired of people telling me what to do," he announced one day. "As soon as I graduate, I'm joining the Marines."

— DENNIS BRESNAHAN

A **s new** Naval reservists, my friends and I were proud to wear our uniforms to an armed-forces parade in New York City. After leaving the subway, we were walking the short distance to the assembly point when we noticed the green coat, gold buttons, and double bars of an approaching officer. We quickly straightened up and presented him with sharp salutes. Our wonder over why the Army captain had not returned our salutes quickly turned to embarrassment when we realized he was a foreman for the New York City sanitation department.

— EDWARD T. ZAREK

V **isiting** Annapolis, I noticed several plebes on their hands and knees holding pencils and clipboards. "What are they doing?" I asked our tour guide.

"Each year, the upperclassmen ask the freshmen how many bricks it took to finish paving this courtyard," he said.

"So what's the answer?" my friend asked.

The guide replied, "One."

— JEROME DASSO

Sign posted in the Army recruiting office:
Marry a veteran, girls. He can cook, make beds, and sew, and is already used to taking orders.

— BRIAN DION

F **ifteen years** of blissful civilian life ended when I re-upped with the Air National Guard recently. It took time to get back into the swing of things, and after a particularly rough day I missed chow, which meant dinner would be a dreaded MRE: Meal Ready-to-Eat. As I sat on my bunk staring at "dinner," I said to a far younger airman, "Well, I guess we just have to get used to roughing it."

"Dude, tell me about it," he said. "We only get basic cable!"

— KINGSLEY SLOANE

While serving as chief medical officer at Fort Ritchie in Maryland, I attended a nearby wedding. Since it was a formal affair at a country club, I went in my officers dress blue uniform.

Once at the club, I drove up to the entrance, where the doorman promptly came to the passenger door and assisted my wife out of the car. He then made his way to my side. But before I could get out, he pointed to the other end of the building and said, "The band entrance is that way."

— GORDON VANOTTEREN

Military guys can't help debating which branch is the best. A friend was asked why he chose the Air Force over the Navy. "Simple, really," he said. "Whatever goes up must come down. But whatever goes down doesn't necessarily have to come up."

— JESSE DAVIS

The guard in Air Force basic training must check the ID of everyone who comes to the door. A trainee was standing guard when he heard a pounding on the door and the order "Let me in!" Through the window he saw the uniform of a lieutenant colonel and immediately opened up. He quickly realized his mistake.

"Airman! Why didn't you check for my authority to enter?"

Thinking fast, the airman replied, "Sir, you'd have gotten in anyway."

"What do you mean?"

"Uh, the hinges on the door. They're broken, sir."

"What? Show me!"

With a twinkle in his eye, the airman opened the door, let the officer step out, and slammed the door shut. "Airman! Open up immediately!"

"Sir, may I see your authority to enter?" The airman was rewarded for outsmarting his commanding officer.

— ROSS BALFOUR

During Army basic training, our first lieutenant took us on a march and asked each of us where our home was. After everyone had answered, he sneered and said, "You're all wrong. The Army is now your home." Back at the barracks, he read our evening duties, then asked our first sergeant if he had anything to say.

"You bet I do," the sergeant replied. "Men, while you were gone today, I found beds improperly made, clothes not hanging correctly, shoes not

"And this is a crossword puzzle I'm working on."

shined, and footlockers a mess. Where do you think you are? Home?"

— **JACK HEAVEY**

Our sergeant major was dimmer than a dying lightning bug. One day, I found a set of dog tags with his name on them in the shower. So, of course, I returned them. "Wow!" he said. "How'd you know they were mine?"

— **JOSE RODRIGUEZ**

My father served in the Seabees, which meant he was more likely to handle a cement mixer than a rifle. I tried to explain this to my six-year-old son.

"Grandpa didn't fight in any battles," I said. "He wasn't that kind of soldier."

"Oh," said my son. "He was in the Salvation Army."

— **JODI WEBB**

One day a young Air Force enlisted man walked into the base newspaper office where I work and said he'd like to place an advertisement. "Classified?" I asked.

"No, ma'am," he replied with great seriousness. "It's unclassified."

— **MONICA COSTELLO**

It was 1943—the height of World War II. *Reader's Digest* ran these examples of military slang "to help us understand Johnny's new lingo for when he comes marching home."

- Armored cow:
  Canned milk
- China clipper:
  Dishwasher
- Roll up your flaps:
  Stop talking
- Side arms:
  Cream and sugar

— RD

The colonel who served as inspector general in our command paid particular attention to how personnel wore their uniforms. On one occasion he spotted a junior airman with a violation. "Airman," he bellowed, "what do you do when a shirt pocket is unbuttoned?"

The startled airman replied, "Button it, sir!"

The colonel looked him in the eye and said, "Well?"

At that, the airman nervously reached over and buttoned the colonel's shirt pocket.

— G. DEARING JR.

When I was an infantry platoon commander, my Marines trained regularly for nighttime reconnaissance patrol. As we moved along, each of us would whisper the name of any obstacle to the person behind so that no one would be surprised and utter a cry that would disclose our position.

During one exercise, the lead man in the formation occasionally turned around and whispered to me "Log" or "Rock," which I would pass along.

Suddenly there was a crash ahead of me and, from several feet down, I heard a single whispered word— "Hole."

— MIKE ROBBINS

My father was serving in a port city in post–World War II Germany when a ship laden with GIs docked. As the soldiers disembarked, they started to jeer and boo. The reason? The local band hired to

A sign your child has been raised in a military family: My daughter was playing with Barbie dolls. Seeing a lone Ken doll among all those women, I said, "Poor Ken, he's the only guy." "Yeah," she said. "All the rest of the dads are deployed."

— MELINDA KUNZ

greet them was playing a popular hit of the time, "I Wonder Who's Kissing Her Now."

— DIANE BENEDICT

We were asleep in our cots at Bagram Air Base in Afghanistan when exploding enemy rockets woke us up. My platoon and I threw on our fatigues, grabbed our weapons, and ran to the bunker for protection.

Inside the bunker, a nervous soldier lit up.

"Put that cigarette out!" I ordered.

"Yeah, forget the rockets," said another soldier as more rounds rocked the bunker. "That secondhand smoke'll kill ya."

— SSG JAMES KELLERT

Our ship had been on deployment in the Red Sea for several months when we made a port stop in Dubai, United Arab Emirates. The weapons officer gathered all the spare change he could find to use the pay phone on the jetty. He waited his turn in line, fed his money into the phone, and dialed home. His seven-year-old answered and said, "Hi, Dad. Where are you?"

The officer replied, "Dubai."

His son said, "OK," then hung up.

— DOUG SCATTERGOOD

My Afghan interpreter loved using American idioms, even though he rarely had a firm grasp of them. One day, during a meeting with village elders, I

Aboard a troop carrier crossing the Atlantic, I noticed a seasick pal of mine losing it over the railing alongside several other soldiers.

"I never knew you had such a weak stomach," I said.

"It's not weak," he replied. "I'm throwing up just as far as the rest of these guys."

— GEORGE MAHATHY

asked him to leave out the chitchat and get to the point.

"I understand, sir," he said. "You want me to cut the cheese."

— PATRICK HAWS

In Iraq, my sergeant was not happy with the speed with which I was moving MREs (Meals Ready-to-Eat) from a non-air-conditioned building into an air-conditioned tent.

"Hurry up," he yelled. "The sun's going to ruin those MREs. Have you ever had a bad MRE?"

Moving a pallet, I grunted, "You ever had a good one?"

— CHRIS NEWTON

THE GREAT PUSHBALL INCIDENT

These Navy boys go to
great lengths to get their ball back.

By Daniel V. Gallery, *Rear Admiral, USN*

Not long after I was sent to Iceland in December 1941 to command a U.S. Fleet air base that was to help the British Navy and Royal Air Force protect convoys, a shipment of recreational equipment arrived. Opening up the boxes like a bunch of kids on Christmas morning, we found, among other things, a pushball, which we promptly blew up to its full five-foot diameter. Exploring the boxes for more loot, we left the pushball sitting outside the gymnasium door unattended.

You should never leave anything as big and light as a pushball unattended in Iceland, because the wind comes along and blows it away. This happened to our pushball. I came out of the gym just in time to watch it bounce down the hill, over a bluff, and into the water. It sailed rapidly across the inlet and grounded on the opposite shore, where a British anti-aircraft battery had its camp.

I wanted that pushball back, so I picked up my telephone to call the commanding officer of the British battery. Strange things often happened on our field telephone system, which consisted of a labyrinth of wires laid out on the ground. This time connections got crossed, and I heard my friend across the way calling British Admiralty Headquarters. "The biggest bloody mine you've ever seen has just washed ashore," he was shouting. "Please send a bomb-disposal party to deal with it!"

I hung up without saying a word and called Admiralty Headquarters myself. I reported that we had seen a mine wash ashore, that we had a qualified bomb-disposal squad, and that if the Admiralty wished us to do so we would be glad to deal with the situation. The Admiralty, of course, was delighted to have somebody take this nasty job off their hands. They promptly replied that this would be "quite satisfactory."

Rounding up about a dozen helpers, I explained the pitch. We organized a bomb-disposal squad on the spot. We grabbed a portable field telephone set, a couple of voltmeters, a stethoscope, and some small toolboxes, and we jeeped over to the British camp. There we found our allies nervously eyeing the "mine" from a respectful distance.

The arrival of our businesslike experts obviously relieved the tension. We had all read enough about bomb disposal to go through the proper motions. We immediately stationed sentries and pushed the crowd back to a safer distance. Then we placed one field telephone at the "mine" and the other a hundred yards back, so that the mine-disposal boys could phone back every move they made, to be recorded in a notebook for the guidance of future mine-disposal squads, in case this one made a wrong move and blew itself up.

After a few minutes of hocus-pocus with the stethoscope and voltmeters, and much telephoning back and forth, we finally gave the signal that the big moment was at hand. As the crowd watched in awed silence we unscrewed the valve, let the air out—and got the hell out of that camp as fast as we could.

Needless to say, this incident helped us immeasurably in getting acquainted with the British.

"Good god, man, flap harder!"

As a flight instructor, one of my duties was to check out pilots who had been involved in aircraft accidents to ensure that they were proficient in emergency procedures. After completing one ride with a helicopter pilot whose engine had failed, the engine on my own helicopter suddenly gave out. As I initiated an emergency landing, I instructed my student to put out a mayday call on the radio.

"Would you rather I take the controls?" he suggested. "After all, I've done this before."
— DANIEL M. JUNEAU

After a snowstorm buried our neighborhood, my wife called the hospital and said she could not make it to work because all the roads were blocked.

"We'll send the National Guard," she was told. "They'll get you out."

"Good luck with that," she said. "My husband's in the National Guard, and he can't get out either."
— BRIAN WOOLSHLEGER

No one on my uncle's troop ship was particularly upset when a much-loathed sergeant went overboard.

No one except the captain. "How did this happen?" he demanded, as the sergeant dried off.

"That's the wrong question, sir," yelled a sailor. "Try asking him whether he was pushed or shoved."

— MALCOLM ELVY

While serving on the USS Fulton (AS-11), in New London, Connecticut, a fellow sailor and I were topside. He leaned over the railing and opened his mouth to say something. As he did, his uppers fell out and sank to the bottom of the Thames River. He didn't seem too bothered, though. "That's OK," he said. "My serial number's engraved on them."

— PAVEL WILSON

We had just moved to an Army post from an Air Force base and my young son, an avid fan of GI Joe toys, was excited to see the troops marching in cadence. An even bigger thrill came when he passed the motor pool with its tanks, jeeps, and trucks. "Look," he squealed with delight. "They have the whole collection!"

— JEREMY THORNTON

After spending a few years on shore duty, I found myself back at sea trying to remember what all of the signal bells and whistles piped over the ship's intercom meant. I was beginning to catch on again when I heard an unfamiliar beeping in the chief's mess. "What's that one?" I asked. When my coworkers finally stopped laughing, they informed me it was the microwave.

— MELANIE M. PATTERSON

Timeless Humor from the '60s

■

Two of my shipmates and I survived a World War II ship sinking by clinging to half of a life raft for three days. One of my buddies had a compound fracture of his right leg, but complained very little of pain. When we were picked up and put in sick bay, the doctor, unaware of our ordeal, examined the fractured leg and commented, "This looks very good, and there's no sign of infection. What treatment was given?"

Without hesitation, my buddy answered, "I've been soaking it in saltwater for the last three days."

— PRESTON A. PRUITT

The scale at our clinic in Iraq was pitiful. Just to get it working properly required plenty of kicking and stomping. One day, as I was going through my weighing-in routine, a medic walked by. Watching as I pounded the scale with my feet, he wondered aloud, "Killing the messenger?"

— **DAWN NEHLS**

Life on board an aircraft carrier is noisy, with jets, mechanical equipment, and the dull roar of blowers circulating air. One night the ship had a massive power failure, and our berthing compartment became abruptly quiet. Everyone woke up with a start. One half-asleep seaman shouted, "What the heck was that?"

From across the dark room came a voice: "That was silence, you idiot!"

— **JAMES TODHUNTER**

It was the '60s, and our unit command decided to let us have mustaches, something our first sergeant clearly opposed. Nevertheless, he told us to go ahead and grow one. A week later, he appeared before the morning formation with a razor. He proceeded to shave off each of our mustaches and let the hairs fall into individual envelopes on which he wrote our name. "Now," he announced, "if anyone asks where your mustache is, tell him it's in the sergeant's safe."

— **GARY MUFFIT**

My son, Barry, came home from a three-month deployment aboard his submarine, and told us that one of the ways the sailors kept up morale was to make wooden cars out of kits and run derby races. "What do you do for a ramp?"" my husband inquired.

"Don't need one," Barry said. "We just put the cars on the floor and then tilt the sub."

— **MARY C. RYAN**

After being at sea in the Persian Gulf for 90 straight days, I went to the squadron command master chief to complain. "Chief, I joined the Navy to see the world," I said, "but for the past three months all I've seen is water."

"Lieutenant," he replied, "three-quarters of the earth is covered with water, and the Navy has been showing you that. If you wanted to see the other quarter, you should have joined the Army."

— **PAUL NEWMAN**

"The war games are going well, sir. We've just reached level four, where our M-16s turn into fire-breathing, tank-eating dragons."

After joining the Navy, my husband underwent a physical. During the exam, the doctor discovered that, due to a bum shoulder, my husband couldn't fully extend his arms above his head. Perplexed, the doctor conferred with another physician. "Let him pass," said the second doctor. "I don't see any problems unless he has to surrender."

— BETTY LEE

My husband was a Navy chaplain deployed to the Persian Gulf at the end of Desert Storm. I did everything possible to ensure that our three young children wouldn't be worried about their father being in danger. It wasn't always easy, but I knew I'd succeeded when someone at church asked our three-year-old where his dad was. My son replied, "He's in Persia, golfing."

— MARSHA HANSEN

An annual survey among my fellow junior officers indicated that lack of communication from our superiors was a big problem. The commanding officer, however, refused to believe the results. "If communication is really so bad," he demanded of his department heads, "why am I only hearing about it now?"

— RICKEY RUFFIN

My cousin, a senior airman in the Air Force, and my brother-in-law, a Marine sergeant, were comparing their experiences in the Saudi Arabian desert. They commiserated about the heat, sand, and food. But when my Air Force cousin grumbled about the uncomfortable beds and the small tents, my Marine brother-in-law looked surprised. His astonishment grew as my cousin went on to complain about the unreliable air-conditioning and meager choice of cable channels. Finally the Marine spoke up: "Tents? You had tents?"

— A.K. MCNEILL

I didn't enlist in the Army—I was drafted. So I wasn't going to make life easy for anyone. During my physical, the doctor asked softly, "Can you read the letters on the wall?" "What letters?" I answered slyly. "Good," said the doctor. "You passed the hearing test."

— ROBERT DUPREY

"Gesundheit."

After my husband, a veteran, spoke at an elementary school, a student asked what he ate during battle.

"C rations," he replied.

"Ooh!" she squealed. "I love seafood."

— **DOTTY BOEZINGER**

While scrubbing the decks of our Coast Guard cutter on a scorching summer day, a few shipmates and I decided to break the rules and go for a swim. With no officers in sight, I scrambled atop a railing 40 feet above the water. Just as I leaned forward, I could see the captain step out on the bridge. Too late to stop, I did a picture-perfect dive into the ocean. When I had clambered back aboard, the captain was there to greet me. Fearing the worst, I was greatly relieved when he said, "I'll give you a ten."

"Thanks, Captain," I said. "I used to dive in college."

"I don't mean a score of ten," he spat back. "I mean ten days of restriction."

— **RUSTY JACKSON**

I WANTED TO JOIN THE ARMY. THE SIGN SAID "BE ALL THAT YOU CAN BE." THEY TOLD ME IT WASN'T ENOUGH.

— JAY LONDON

Whoever said the pen is mightier than the sword obviously never encountered automatic weapons.

— GEN. DOUGLAS MACARTHUR

I was in the Army, and to me it was like a newsreel.

— MEL BROOKS.

Seeing your name on the list for KP or guard duty when you're in the Army is like reading a bad review.

— ROBERT DUVAL

Nothing in life is so exhilarating as to be shot at without result.

— WINSTON CHURCHILL

I was in the ROTC. Of course, ROTC stood for 'Running off to Canada.'

— JAY LENO

Leaders can let you fail and yet not let you be a failure.

—GEN. STANLEY MCCHRYSTAL

Success is how high you bounce when you hit bottom.

— GEN. GEORGE S. PATTON

When I lost my rifle, the Army charged me $85. That's why in the Navy, the captain goes down with the ship.

— DICK GREGORY

YOU, YOU, AND YOU... PANIC. THE REST OF YOU, COME WITH ME.

— U.S. MARINE CORPS GUNNERY SERGEANT

FEELING THE HEAT

The brass had a chilly reaction
to his warm-hearted gesture.

By Tom C. McKenney

Near the end of the Korean War, I was a young Marine officer serving in the outpost line. Winter, with its -25°F nights, was coming on, and our battalion chaplain thought we could help the people in the local village by asking friends and family back home for donations of warm clothing.

A gung-ho second lieutenant named Dudley Floren wrote to his parents, passing along the chaplain's request. As an afterthought, Dudley suggested they send everything collect, and he would pay the postage.

Next, Dudley took the project a giant leap further: He wrote to his brother Myron Floren, a star accordion player who regularly performed on *The Lawrence Welk Show*, to appeal for donations during his next TV appearance. Dudley reminded his brother to say that all postage would be paid.

Sure enough, packages of winter clothing began to pile up at the battalion postal tent and soon overwhelmed the clerk, who shut down the office. No one in the battalion was getting mail. It got worse. The division's post office was inundated, too, and promptly shut down, so no one in the entire First Marines could get any mail.

Dudley had to answer first to the battalion commander, then the regiment commander, and finally the commanding general. Desperate, he wrote Myron again, urging him to tell TV viewers to stop the donations, but it could take a month for a letter to reach home. Meanwhile, the clothes kept coming and Dudley's postal bill kept climbing. It hit $24,000—at a time when a second lieutenant's base pay was $222 a month.

I'll never forget the sight of that hill of unwanted coats outside the command post covered with snow.

FUNNY
FURRY
FRIENDS

I had an inauspicious start as a dog groomer when one of my first clients bit me. Noticing my pain, my boss voiced her concern.

"Whatever you do," she said, "don't bleed on the white dogs."

— JAN VIRGO

When a lonely frog consults a fortune-teller, he's told not to worry. "You are going to meet a beautiful young girl," she says, "and she will want to know everything about you."

"That's great!" says the excited frog. "When will I meet her?"

"Next semester," says the psychic, "in biology class."

— ZHANG WENYI

An adorable little girl walked into my pet shop and asked, "Excuse me, do you have any rabbits here?"

"I do," I answered, and, leaning down to her eye level, I asked, "Did you want a white rabbit or would you rather have a soft, fuzzy black rabbit?"

She shrugged. "I don't think my python really cares."

— CINDY PATTERSON

Friends of mine sold their country home to move to the city after arranging for the new owners to keep their dog, which they said was an excellent watch dog.

On their first night in the city, they received a frantic phone call from the new owners.

"Please come back and collect your dog," they begged. "We've been out for the day and it won't let us back onto the property."

— NORMA KAWACK

There, in the reptiles section of our zoo, a male turtle was on top of a female behaving very, um, affectionately. My daughter was transfixed. She asked, "Mommy?"

Uh-oh, I thought. Here comes The Question. "Yes?" I said.

"Why doesn't he go around?"

— DAWN HOISINGTON

My greatest contribution to humor came when I taught my pet lizard to walk on its hind legs. It was the world's first stand-up chameleon.
— JOHN S. CROSBIE

A **mother** mouse and her baby were scampering across a polished floor when they heard a noise. They hoped it would be a human being, but it turned out to be the family cat. Upon seeing the mice, the cat gave chase. Mama mouse felt a swipe of paw and claw. She turned in her tracks and called out in her loudest voice, "Bow-wow!" and the cat ran off.

Gathering her baby to her and catching her breath, Mama mouse explained, "Now, my child, you see how important a second language is."

— SANDRA J. HULDEN

A **guy finds** a sheep wandering in his neighborhood and takes it to the police station. The desk sergeant says, "Why don't you just take it to the zoo?"

The next day, the sergeant spots the same guy walking down the street—with the sheep.

"I thought I told you to take that sheep to the zoo," the sergeant says.

"I know what you told me," the guy responds. "Yesterday I took him to the zoo. Today I'm taking him to the movies."

— TAMARA CUMMINGS

A **lonely** woman buys a parrot for companionship. After a week the parrot hasn't uttered a word, so the woman goes back to the pet store and buys it a mirror. Nothing. The next week, she brings home a little ladder. Polly is still incommunicado,

My wife found this flyer taped to a neighborhood telephone pole:

Found, male yellow Lab, very friendly. Loves to play with kids and eat Bubbles. Bubbles is our cat. Please come get your dog.

— ROBERT CHAPMAN

so the week after that, she gives it a swing, which elicits not a peep. A week later she finds the parrot on the floor of its cage, dying. Summoning up its last breath, the bird whispers, "Don't they have any food at that pet store?"

— LUCILLE ARNELL

Then there was the old gal who died and left $20,000 to her dog and cat.

"But they're going to have trouble trying to collect." said one chap, "I understand her parakeet is contesting the will."

— CHRIS HOBSON

"Yes, I'm still paying off the china shop
incident. Any other questions, Mr. Nosy?"

As I was walking through a variety store, I stopped at the pet department to look at some parakeets. In one cage a green bird lay on his back, one foot hooked oddly into the cage wire. I was about to alert the saleswoman to the bird's plight when I noticed a sign taped to the cage: "No, I am not sick. No, I am not dead. No, my leg is not stuck in the cage. I just like to sleep this way."

— JOAN DEZEEUW

I was editing classified ads for a small-town newspaper when a man called to place an ad.

"It should read," he said, "'Free to good home. Golden retriever. Will eat anything, loves children.'"

— ELLEN YOUNG

A friend of mine received a pet ferret as a gift from his girlfriend. This small, weasel-like creature is very tame, but it's small wonder that heads turn when the adorable animal is walked on its leash along the city streets. Its name? Ferret Fawcett, of course!

— TIMOTHY STEWART

Cat Person
∎

If you nod knowingly at these tweets, you're a cat person:

I like to sleep on the left side of the bed, and my cat likes to sleep on the left side of the bed. So we compromised, and I sleep on the right side of the bed.
— @JULIETROUGE

I feel like 90 percent of having a cat is saying, "Where is the cat?"
— @THE_RUG

A guy I was dating sat down on the couch next to me. I proceeded to whisper "That's the cat's spot" to myself.
— @CHRISTYSHARK89

Sometimes I'll ask my cats, "Are you a good kitty?" They just look at me, and my wife will say, "Answer your father."
— @TASTEFACTORY

Sounds of crashing and banging in the middle of the night sent me and my husband out to our garage. There we spotted three raccoons eating out of the cat dish. We shooed them away and went back to bed.

Later that week we were driving home and I noticed three fat raccoons ambling down the road. "Do you think those are the same ones we chased off?" I asked.

"Hard to tell," said my husband. "They were wearing masks."

— CHERIE KONVICKA

A talking horse shows up at Dodger Stadium and persuades the manager to let him try out for the team.

In his first at bat, the horse rips the ball deep into right field— then just stands there.

"Run! Run!" the manager screams.

"Run?" says the horse. "If I could run, I'd be in the Kentucky Derby."

— CHARLES LEERSHEN

The injury to our piglet wasn't serious, but it did require stitches. So I sent my teenage daughter back into the farmhouse to get needle and thread and bring it to me, while I looked after the squealing animal.

Ten minutes later she still hadn't returned.

"What are you doing?" I called out.

She yelled back, "Looking for the pink thread!"

— JUNE HALEY

I worked at a boarding kennel, where people leave their dogs and cats while on vacation. One morning I had taken a cat out of his cage, and after playing with him and replenishing his food and water, I put him back in. A few minutes later, I was

Timeless Humor from the '40s

■

On a hunting trip in the north woods, we stayed at a lodge run by an old guide who had lived alone in the wilds most of his life, with only about a dozen dogs of various breeds and sizes for companions. It was very cold, and the first evening one of the men, noticing the scant bed covering, asked what we should do if we got cold in the night.

"Wal," the old guide replied, taking a long draw on his pipe, "just pull up another dawg."

— WILBUR R. PERRY

"Master, Rex wants to know if you're through playing with his stick."

surprised to see the feline at my feet, since the cage doors lock automatically when they're shut. I couldn't figure out how the cat escaped, until I bent down to pick him up and spied his name tag: Houdini.

— BARBARA ROHRSSEN

On a recent trip to the post office, I took a few minutes to read the notices posted on the public bulletin board in the lobby. One in particular caught my eye.

It read, "Lost in post office parking lot, small boa constrictor, family pet, will not attack. Reward."

Below the notice someone had written, in what appeared to be very shaky handwriting: "Please, would you mind posting another notice when you find your boa? Thank you."

— SUSAN EBENSON

I think my goldfish has seizures," a man tells the veterinarian.

"He seems fine now," says the vet.

"Now, sure. But wait till I take him out of the bowl."

— NANCY SEND

A **farmer pulls** a prank on Easter Sunday. After the egg hunt he sneaks into the chicken coop and replaces every white egg with a brightly colored one.

Minutes later the rooster walks in. He spots the colored eggs, then storms out and beats up the peacock.

— ADAM JOSHUA SMARGON

L **ate one** afternoon on the London Underground, I found myself sitting next to a man who held an empty birdcage on his lap. Curiosity prompted me to ask if the bird had escaped.

"Oh, no," the man replied. "You see, my working hours are irregular, and we have no telephone in our home, so my wife never knows when to expect me for dinner. I take my homing pigeon along to work every morning and release it as soon as my job is finished.

"Dinner'll be ready when I get home," he concluded.

— OIVIND HOLTAN

M **y young** son and I spent much time in pet shops looking for just the right fish for his aquarium and for snails to keep the tank clean. One day he came home from a shopping trip all excited to tell me he had discovered some African frogs that really did a good job cleaning the aquarium.

"Good," I said, "then you won't have to buy any snails."

"Oh, yes," he said, "I have to buy them too. Those frogs don't do windows."

— MRS. ROGER RAYMOND

S **cientists** at the University of Pennsylvania School of Medicine announced they have found a cure for baldness in mice. This is great news. Nothing looks more ridiculous than a mouse with a comb-over.

— BEN WALSH

M **y sister's** children finally got their turn to take home the school's incredibly long-lived guinea pig, Peter. After

My sight-impaired friend was in a grocery store with her guide dog when the manager asked, "Is that a blind dog?" My friend said, "I hope not, or we're both in trouble."

— SUE YOUNG

enjoying his company for a few days, my sister was horrified to find Peter dead one morning. She and her husband hid the cage and dashed to the pet store, intent on replacing the guinea pig before anyone was any the wiser.

The pet-store owner listened carefully to their description of Peter's markings. "You're looking for the St. Peter's school guinea pig. I think I have another one," he said calmly. "You're not the first, you know. Guinea pigs don't live very long."

— CAROL ENGELBERTS

One afternoon I was walking on a trail with my newborn daughter, chatting to her about the scenery. When a man and his dog approached, I leaned into the baby carriage and said, "See the doggy?"

Our daughter was working as a telemarketer for a home-security firm. Once while she was reciting all the benefits of the system to a potential customer, he interrupted her and said, "We don't need it because we have a big dog."

"That's great," my daughter replied. "But can he dial 911?"

— EVELYN DREEBEN

Suddenly I felt a little silly talking to my baby as if she understood me. But just as the man passed, I noticed he reached down, patted his dog and said, "See the baby?"

— CATHERINE REARDON

My six-year-old loved his pet fish. He watched and fed it faithfully, morning and night. But one day while he was in school, his fish died, so I flushed it down the toilet. I told him when he got home, and he was inconsolable. Nothing I said helped. After a while, I asked, "Why are you crying so much?"

Arching his back, he shouted, "I wanted to flush!"

— JUDITH PARNETT

What is that sound?" a woman visiting our nature center asked.

"It's the frogs trilling for a mate," Patti, the naturalist, explained. "We have a pair in the science room. But since they've been together for so long, they no longer sing to each other."

The woman nodded sympathetically. "The trill is gone."

— KATHYJO TOWNSON

THE COMPANY WE KEEP

A houseful of guests is always fun. But when they happen to be birds and wild animals, anything can occur.

By John and Jean George

arly one morning we were called to a Poughkeepsie, New York, police station near our home to claim our Canada goose and mallard duck.

The desk sergeant read us a memorandum: "Picked up at 3 a.m. walking down the middle of College Avenue making loud sqwanks and quacks." Then he added, seriously, "Looks like a clear-cut case of vagrancy and disturbing the peace."

"Not guilty," said John, equally serious. "They were just calling their mother."

"And where was their mother?" asked the officer.

"He was home in bed."

"He! What do you mean, he?"

"I mean that I am a mother goose!" John stated with some pride. "Nothing in this world would convince that gosling that I am not. You see, I helped her out of her eggshell. I was the first moving thing she saw, and to a hatching bird that is always 'mother.' Animal behaviorists call this 'imprinting.' She doesn't know she's a goose and wouldn't recognize a goose if she saw one. Her idea of a goose is me. The duck, on the other hand, thinks he is a goose; the goose was the first thing he responded to on hatching.

"Last night something awakened the gosling, and she needed to know whether to be frightened or to go back to sleep. So she went out to look for me, calling as she went. The duck went with her because he thinks she is his mother, and since she was calling he thought he ought to call too."

"Well, now," said the officer, "I don't know of any law that states that a gosling can't look for its mother. Case dismissed."

To become a mother goose gives one insight into the life of the gosling that cannot be gained by a thousand trips into the wilderness to study geese. We need such insight because we write and illustrate books about wild birds and mammals, so every time we start another animal biography we bring the principal characters into our home. This may seem a hectic way to get the animal point of view, but it is rewarding.

Jean learned what it would be like to see in the dark through the eyes of a guest in our home—a fox named Fulva. Every night in the inky blackness of the yard, Jean and Fulva played with a tennis ball. It was a one-sided game. Jean could not see Fulva, much less the ball. A wet nose would touch her hand, and a ball would be pressed there. Jean would throw it. There would be only the sound of the ball bouncing on the earth. Soon the wet nose would touch her again, and the ball would be in her hand.

"To look and look and see only blackness," Jean recalls, "and to be aware that your fellow player sees not only you, but the ball, the insects, and the stirring leaves, makes you feel terribly limited."

Fulva never got her sexes mixed, as the goose did, and said as much by biting all men—including John—and playing with all women. John was unhappy in his role as enemy of a fox and did not cheer up until spring, when Falco, the male sparrow hawk, fell in love with him.

The hawk courted John according to the rules of the bird world. Having staked off the kitchen, where his nest box was nailed above the door, he defended his home against all intruders, particularly against Jean. If she came near the door Falco would dive-bomb her with outstretched talons. Consequently John became the cook, and the strange couple had the kitchen to themselves. While the hamburgers sizzled, Falco went through his courtship dance, fanning his wings, bowing, bobbing his head, and emitting soft throaty sounds. John would wave his hands in response and talk to him. Falco, thrilled by these attentions, would sail around the kitchen flashing his wings and calling. This went on for a month. Then a pet crow arrived in our house and Falco abandoned John and flew off into the wilderness.

The crow was named New York by our young son, Craig, because he was "as noisy as New York City." The pet grew and prospered like his namesake and all but ran the house. In the morning he flew in the window, perched on Jean's head, and announced the day. Then he would help himself to any food that we didn't throw ourselves on to protect. He considered the children's toys his natural inheritance. One day Twig, our daughter, came crying to us, saying she wasn't going to play with that crow anymore—he had taken the pieces of her puzzle and hidden them in the apple tree.

In the autumn New York walked the children to the school-bus stop. It would have been easier for him to fly, but a crow is a highly social bird and motivated by what the gang is doing. The only gang he knew walked. So he walked down the road in front of Twig and Craig, strutting and tossing pebbles. Occasionally he startled a neighbor with a gravelly "Hello." When the school bus picked up the children he would fly home and report a job well done to Jean, who was busy at the dishpan. If he attempted to help with this chore she would gather him up—feathers, feet, and squawk —and put him out the door. Then she counted the silver.

Later that autumn, the wild crows discovered New York, and would awaken the neighborhood at five o'clock cawing at him. One November morning he flew off with them and never came back.

> **We released a raccoon in the wood only to find him in the sugar can.**

All our wild guests are free to come and go, and by picking their own moments of departure they have, we feel, a better chance of survival. They usually leave in the spring or fall—times when intense biological drives eclipse their memories of man, or guide them in spite of their poor training.

We acquire our guests while they are quite young, when they become devoted to whoever is caring for them. After they can eat on their own, we generally permit them to go free. The most valuable animals are those that visit the woods and permit us to follow them. We have followed raccoons on fishing trips (the big ones get away from them, too). We have swum underwater with mink.

Some animals we just can't get rid of. We released a raccoon in the woods five times only to come home and find him in the sugar can or happily peeling wallpaper off the walls. We were growing desperate when one February night a female raccoon dropped by and we never saw the young fellow again.

We have learned to work with the nature of the animals. Once a raccoon made off with our car keys and carried them up a 60-foot tree. John started to put on his climbing spurs, but then remembered that raccoons like to carry food and trinkets to water and swish them

around in it. So Jean put the dishpan outdoors on a table and started splashing the water. Down the tree loped the bandit with the keys in his teeth. He bounced onto the table and dunked them in the water.

Animals have found desirable retreats in our home for mysterious reasons. A little screech owl would wait patiently on the turntable of an old windup Victrola for someone to give it a crank and turn it on, sending him spinning. We still don't know what kind of owl joy this brought to him, but he stayed with us for a year persisting in this pleasure.

One does not live closely with animals without understanding some of the laws of the wild, such as the finality of the departure of the young from their parents. One afternoon the fox goes under the fence as if called by an irresistible force, and we know she will not be back. The owl climbs high into a tree and looks fiercely at the horizon. He flies in a determined, steady flight, and we know he is gone.

Encumbered by a human point of view, we look upon these departures with some sadness. There will be no visits home. This is it. But we know, too, that these departures are the seeds of the future—that the wilderness will again burst with young, come another spring.

"Yes, he talks, but he prefers text or e-mail."

My friend has a golden retriever that responds to music, and seems to especially like opera. The dog is appropriately named Poochini.

— JERRY SIMON

Carrying two dead raccoons, a buzzard tries to check in at LAX for the red-eye to New York. "Sorry, sir," says the ticket agent. "We allow only one item of carrion."

— JANET HUGHES

When my daughter and I caught only one perch on our fishing trip—not enough for even a modest lunch—we decided to feed it to her two cats. She put our catch in their dish and watched as the two pampered pets sniffed at the fish but refused to eat it.

Thinking quickly, my daughter then picked up the dish, walked over to the electric can opener, ran it for a few seconds, then put the fish back down. The cats dug right in.

— SUSAN WARD

A turtle is crossing the road when he's mugged by two snails. When the police show up, they ask him what happened. The shaken turtle replies, "I don't know. It all happened so fast."

— DEBBY CARTER

My 18-year-old daughter and I were sitting in the yard one afternoon when our cat sauntered by.

"That cat certainly has a great life," I remarked. "She comes and goes just as she darn well pleases."

"That," my daughter replied dryly, "is because she doesn't live with her mother."

— NANCY SIEGEL

A kangaroo orders a beer. He puts down a $20 bill. The bartender gives him $1 in change and says, "Don't see a lot of kangaroos in here."

"At these prices," says the kangaroo, "I'm not surprised."

— CHARLES LEERSHEN

One woman in our tour group was a strict vegetarian. When she talked about her cat, though, she admitted that she fed her pampered pet expensive canned meats.

"Why is it all right for your cat to eat meat if it isn't for you?" I finally asked her.

"My cat and I don't have the same beliefs," she replied.

— DORA GIGGY

Sorry, I wasn't listening when you were talking about your dog. I was busy looking in my phone for a picture of my superior dog.

— @PRIMAWESOME

As a single parent, I know that my ten-year-old daughter has learned to do without many extras. Some time ago, to make things up to her, I promised to buy her toys as soon as I got a raise. A while later, my boss went on vacation and arranged for me to watch his dog, cats, and parrot.

The night before he was due back, we went to feed the animals for the last time. As my daughter busied herself with the parrot, I couldn't believe my ears. She was bombarding the hapless bird with: "Mommy needs a raise! Mommy needs a raise! Mommy needs a raise!"

I got the raise; she got the toys.

— REGINA WIEGAND

My friend George adopted an adorable but stubborn Australian terrier puppy who refused to be housebroken.

Frustrated, George signed them both up for expensive obedience classes.

Recently, I saw man and pup out for a walk and asked how the training went.

"Well," George said, "I don't poop in the house anymore."

— JANE HAMILTON

I held a garage sale with my little blond cairn terrier for company. Soon came the first customer. He took his time browsing and examining everything I had out for sale. Eventually he found something that interested him. "Excuse me," he said. "How much for the dog?"

— MILDRED ROSS DRUM

It was my first year teaching tenth-graders geometry, and I was frustrated with the lack of effort in the class. Trying to make the group more interactive, I asked, "Who can define a polygon?"

"A dead parrot," came the reply.

— JOEL ALMEIDA

A parrot was up for sale at an auction. The bidding proceeded briskly, and soon a winner was announced. When paying, the high bidder asked the auctioneer if the parrot could speak.

"Sure can." replied the auctioneer, "It was the parrot that was bidding against you."

— ANNE H. WINSNES

"I never should have eaten that third license plate."

Driving to work one morning, I heard an announcement on the radio about a lost dog. The deejay said the owner was offering a cash reward for its return. Getting to the traffic segment of his broadcast, the deejay asked the helicopter pilot who monitors morning rush hour what the roads were like. "To heck with the traffic," the pilot said on the air, "we're going to look for that dog!"

— SUZANNE DOPP

After we moved to the country, our cat, Sadie, became a particularly good mouser. I praised her efforts, and she began leaving the mice in conspicuous places so my husband could dispose of them. Along the way, Sadie even developed a good understanding of men. One morning, courtesy of Sadie, my husband found a dead mouse lying on the sofa next to the television remote control.

— BARBARA DIANNIBELLA

They say that a black cat brings bad luck. Is that true?"

"Depends on who comes across it: a human, or a mouse."

— CHAYAN

Our curiosity was aroused by our neighbors' parakeet, whose raucous warnings, "No hand-holding! No kissing!" shattered the quiet of their living room. He'd been trained, our friends explained, to chaperone their teenage daughter's parties.

—MAUD NOBRIGA

The kids had been begging for weeks, so their mom finally gave in and bought them a hamster. But, just as she had feared, she was the one who wound up taking care of it. One evening, exasperated, she sat them down and asked,

"Why did you even want that darn thing? How many times do you think it would have died if I hadn't been looking after it for you?"

"I don't know," her son said. "Once?"

— ADAM JOSHUA SMARGON

I had just come out of a store when the blast of a car horn scared me. When I turned to yell at the rude driver, I found a large white poodle sitting in the driver's seat of a parked car. When the impatient dog honked again, a man came scurrying out of a nearby shop, shouting, "I'll be there in a minute!"

"Did you teach your dog to do that?" I asked the man.

"Yes," he answered

Timeless Humor from the '50s

■

I often passed a house where two little boys of about eight and ten lived. They invariably came dashing out to pet my dog and they seemed to have such fun with him that I asked, "Didn't you ever have a dog of your own?"

They shook their heads. "Dad won't let us."

So I was surprised, a few days later, to find the two youngsters romping on their lawn with a puppy.

"Well," I said, "Dad finally bought you a dog."

The kids grinned. "No, he's Dad's dog. We gave him to Dad for Father's Day—but he lets us play with him."

— E.W. HUTCHINSON

*"OK, when I was a kitten I may have lied
about where I came from."*

in exasperation, "and now he won't let me go anywhere!"

— NANCY E. HAIGH

n the crowded suburban bus, the voice of a six-year-old returning homeward with his mother after a day of shopping rang out loud and clear, "Is our cat a daddy cat or a mother cat?"

"He's a daddy cat," the mother replied patiently.

"How do we know he's a daddy cat?" the boy asked.

An expectant hush fell over the bus, and the passengers listened attentively to see how the mother would handle this one. She was ready for the challenge.

"He's got whiskers, hasn't he?" she said.

— JOE MCCARTHY

NO MATTER HOW MUCH CATS FIGHT, THERE ALWAYS SEEM TO BE PLENTY OF KITTENS.

— ABRAHAM LINCOLN

The cat could very well be man's best friend but would never stoop to admitting it.

— DOUG LARSON

I think there's something great and generic about goldfish. They're everybody's first pet.

— PAUL RUDD

Dogs look up to you; cats look down on you. Give me a pig! He looks you in the eye and treats you as an equal.

— WINSTON CHURCHILL

No animal should ever jump up on the dining room furniture unless absolutely certain that he can hold his own in the conversation.

— FRAN LEBOWITZ

Live in such a way that you would not be ashamed to sell your parrot to the town gossip.

— WILL ROGERS

My roommate got a pet elephant. Then it got lost. It's in the apartment somewhere.

— STEPHEN WRIGHT

I don't believe in reincarnation, and I didn't believe in it when I was a hamster.

— SHANE RITCHIE

I HOPE YOU LOVE BIRDS TOO. IT IS ECONOMICAL. IT SAVES GOING TO HEAVEN.

— EMILY DICKINSON

THE DINGOS ATE MY UNDIES!

Tux and Tweed had a brief stretch as herders.

By Jan Fenimore

Wash day in our small Colorado farming town caused our family some apprehension in 1953. We knew that lingerie regularly disappeared from local clotheslines, swiped in broad daylight. And only our family knew the secret behind the thefts.

Dad owned a ranch about 15 miles from town. Someone told him that dingo-mix dogs were good herders, so he got two of them—Tux and Tweed—to help him and his ranch hands round up the cattle, which they did on horseback.

Every day, Dad took the dogs with him out to the ranch, where he let them run free. He didn't know how to train them, and as a result, the dogs were useless for their intended purpose.

After a time, he left Tux and Tweed home with us when he went to the ranch. With no leash laws, the dogs took to roaming around town.

One day, my little brother ran inside with a shocker: Tweed was chewing on a girdle, and Tux had a bra in his mouth! Mom was mortified by the dogs' antics and was too ashamed to try to find where to return the lingerie.

The dogs got a scolding, but they'd already developed an affinity for pulling women's undergarments off the clotheslines and bringing them home to us.

The thefts continued for weeks, until finally, after trying and failing to keep the dogs from wandering, we found them new homes.

Even in our gossipy town, we never heard mention of the missing unmentionables. We knew we'd never tell.

SAY WHAT?

To celebrate his 40th birthday, my boss, who is battling middle-age spread, bought a new convertible sports car. As a finishing touch, he put on a vanity plate with the inscription "18 Again." The wind was let out of his sails, however, when a salesman entered our office the following week.

"Hey," he called out, "who owns the car with the plate 'I ate again'?"

— CINDY GILLIS

Searching in my local library for two books by communications expert Deborah Tannen turned into an Abbott and Costello routine. "What's the first book?" the librarian asked.

"*That's Not What I Meant!*" I said.

"Well, what did you mean?"

"That's the title of the book," I explained.

"OK." She looked at me a little skeptically. "And the other book?"

"*You Just Don't Understand!*"

"Excuse me?"

I got both books. Eventually.

— NORM WILLIAMS

While redecorating my bathroom, I phoned a shop to see if it stocked a particular model of toilet. "We haven't got one here," said the clerk.

"Oh, no!" I said, crestfallen. His number had been the fourth one I'd called.

"Don't worry," he added helpfully. "I'll contact our other outlets to see if there's anybody out there sitting on one."

— DOUG BINGHAM

We were shopping for clothes when my 13-year-old daughter spotted a hat with

Guinness written on it. She put it on and proclaimed, "Look! I'm a genius!"

— LAURA SANDOVAL

Driving through Southern California, I stopped at a roadside stand that sold fruit, vegetables, and crafts. As I went to pay, I noticed that the young woman behind the counter was painting a sign.

"Why the new sign?" I asked.

"My boyfriend didn't approve of the old one," she said. When I glanced at what hung above the counter, I understood. It declared: "Local Honey Dates Nuts."

— THEODORE BOLOGNA

I returned from Russia after living there nearly two years. My sister decided to surprise me by creating welcome home signs in

Russian. She went to a website that offered translations and typed in "Welcome Home, Cole." She then printed the translated phrase onto about 20 colored cardboard signs.

When I got off the plane, the first thing I saw was my family, excitedly waving posters printed with a strange message. My sister gave me a big hug and pointed proudly to her creations. "Isn't that great?" she said. "Bet you didn't think I knew any Russian."

I admitted that I was indeed surprised— and so was she when I told her what the signs actually said: "Translation not found."

— COLE M. CRITTENDEN

On a trip to a rural Irish village, a friend of mine stopped off at the only shop in town to buy a newspaper. However, all it had was the previous day's edition. "Excuse me," he asked the shop owner, "do you have today's newspaper?"

"Yes, I do," answered the man. "It'll be here tomorrow."

—H.H.

My coworker was very excited at the prospect of becoming an American citizen after passing her test and interview.

"I just have one more thing to do," Pam said proudly. "I have to go to the courthouse in a few weeks and swear at the judge!"

— YEFIM M. BRODD

I could sense that something was bothering my mother,

My colleagues and I recently received this e-mail from the facilities department: "Due to construction, your office may be either cooler or warmer than usual on Tuesday. Dress accordingly."

— DEBRA DONATH

so I asked her if anything was wrong.

"Yes," she admitted. "What's all this I hear on the news about banning baking products?"

I patted her hand reassuringly and said, "That's vaping products."

— JOSEPH MCLAUGHLIN

My professor once went to hear French philosopher Jacques Derrida speak. The entire talk was about cows; everyone was flummoxed but listened carefully and took notes about … cows. There was a short break, and when Derrida came back, he announced, "I'm told it is pronounced 'chaos.'"

— @PMGENTRY

During a train ride in Italy, my new husband and I chatted up an elderly couple with the help of our trusty Italian phrase book. I quietly practiced the pronunciation for "We are on our honeymoon," then confidently exclaimed "*Siamo allupato!*" The couple's jaws dropped and the blood drained from their faces. I rechecked the book and realized I had told this lovely couple that we were—how should I put this?—in an amorous mood. From then on, my husband held on to the book.

— ANDREA PALUMBO

My first job was at a fine-dining establishment. On the night we ran out of french fries, my boss handed me $100 and told me to run to the McDonald's next door and get $100 worth of fries. But when I came back with two huge greasy sacks, my boss looked confused.

"What's this?" she asked. "The $100 worth of fries you asked for," I said.

Her eyes narrowed. "I told you $100 in fives!"

— KELLY SEMB

Tiffany adopts two dogs, and she names them Rolex and Timex. "Where'd you come up with those names?" asks her friend Mandy.

"HellOOOOOO," Tiffany replies. "They're watchdogs!"

— GUSTAVO YEPES

Timeless Humor from the '30s
■

Neither my thoughts nor my eyes were on the familiar road that morning, when—*crash*! My car had locked bumpers with another in the middle of a one-way bridge. By the time a state patrolman arrived, a line of impatient motorists had formed on each end of the bridge. After asking the usual questions he said to me: "So you're an English professor!"

Turning to the crowd he commanded, "Stand back, folks. I got business with this fellow." I steeled myself for a lecture on absentmindedness.

"Now ain't this nice!" the patrolman began. "All my life there's been a matter I've been waitin' to ask one of you professors about if I ever run one down. My time's come."

He thrust his face close to mine. "Tell me," he demanded. "What's a split infinitive?"

— WILLIAM PERRY

"It's true—we do have 100 words for snow, but most of them are curse words."

During a high school visit to France, I stayed with a French family. One night, I was unsure what the meat on my dinner plate was, so I pointed to it and asked in my best 11th-grade French: "*Qui est-ce?*" The family's expressions told me I needed some tutoring. Instead of asking "What is it?" as I had intended, I'd asked "Who is it?"

— **BRIGITTE BRULZ**

My four-year-old grandson, Cole, was sounding out words to type into his entertainment gaming system. "Nama," Cole asked me, "how do you spell 'fur'?"

"F-u-r," I said.

"I know how to spell 'Chris,'" he said. "I'm writing 'Christopher.'"

"Oh, let me see," I said, then went over to look at what he had entered.

On the screen was "Chris the Fur"!

— **ROSE BRADY**

My mother would always say "Mind your PBJs"
when she meant to say "Mind your p's and q's."

— KATHRYN SCHULLER

The fur began to fly when my fellow airplane passengers learned there was a chance they might miss their connecting flights out of Aspen. When we finally landed, I found out just how nasty things really got.

Over the intercom, a harried flight attendant announced, "Those of you continuing on to L.A., please wait outside next to the boarding ramp and we will have a shuttle run you over."

— ALAINA WAGNER

Coincidences were flying when a man was arrested and charged with stealing a bird feeder from Cornell University's ornithology laboratory. According to the Associated Press, police charged James Buzzard, 44, who lives on Cardinal Drive in Ithaca, New York, with stealing the feeder from the lab on Sapsucker Woods Road.

— GEROLENE E. SNAVELY

Sitting at a stoplight, I was puzzling over the meaning of the vanity plate on the car in front of me. It read "Innie."

Then I got it. The make of the car was Audi.

— KATHY JOHNSON

Days after posting a bilingual traffic sign in Swansea, Wales, officials were alerted to a problem. The English half was fine, but the Welsh, which had been e-mailed to the translator and returned minutes later, read, when translated back into English, "I am not in the office."

— READER'S DIGEST

When my sister's friend Stephany was caught texting "WTF," she had to think fast. "It means 'With the Family,'" she told her mother. Mom, a social media newbie, bought it.

A few months later, their family took a vacation to Paris, where Stephany's mom gushed, "I can't believe all these Facebook likes I'm getting about our trip."

"Why, what are you saying?" Stephany asked.

"Nothing special. 'In Paris WTF.'"

— AVIAD MATAROSO

"Honey, I'm taking the dog
out to do his business."

A MOMENT WITH MANDY

A noted humorist is entrapped by an eight-year-old in a battle of wits, and emerges—barely.

By James Thurber

Why didn't God make bats butterflies?" Mandy suddenly asked me one day. Her questions demand a grave consideration, which her impatience with the slow processes of the adult mind will not tolerate.

Mandy is eight, but I state her age with reservations because she is sometimes 14 or older, and sometimes four or younger.

"I want to hang by my heels like a bat," Mandy said, "but I want to be a butterfly. Daddy couldn't spank me then because I would be on the ceiling."

"He could get a stepladder," I said finally.

"I would push it over," she said. "*Bang!*"

"He could call the fire department, of course," I suggested.

"I would push that over too," Mandy said, adding, "*Bang, bang!*"

"Butterflies don't hang by their heels," I told her, but she was off on another tack.

"God didn't have to give turtles shells," she told me.

Here I thought I had her, but she does not corner easily in debate. "Turtles are very slow," I explained, "and so God gave them shells they could hide in, to protect themselves from their enemies."

"Why didn't he make them faster?" Mandy said. She had me there. I realized, for the first time, that if God had made porcupines and skunks faster, they wouldn't need their quills and vitriol, respectively.

"Why didn't God give us wings?" was her next question, and I began to lecture on that point.

"We have developed wings," I told her, but she cut me off with that topic sentence.

"It took God a million billion years to give us wings," she said. "They are no good." To this she added, after a moment's thought, "We don't have anything."

"We have better eyesight than dogs," I said.

"Dogs don't bump into things. People bump into things."

"Dogs are guided by better hearing and a better sense of smell than we have," I explained.

"They can't see a light way way off," was her answer to that.

"No, but when the man with the light gets nearer, they can hear him, and then they can smell him," I said.

She left me flat-footed with a quick passing shot. "This light doesn't get nearer, 'cause it's in a lighthouse."

That annoyed me, for I am a bad loser. "All right, all right, then," I snapped. "We'll move the dog nearer the lighthouse. Aren't you going to allow me to score a single point in this colloquy?"

Mandy has a standard answer for any questions she doesn't understand. "No," she said. "Why didn't God give dogs glasses?"

For days I had been practicing some questions of my own for Mandy, and I served them all at once. "Why don't foxes wear foxgloves? Why don't cows wear cowslips? What was it Katy did? If cowboys round up cows, why don't bulldogs round up bulls?"

"Katy who?" Mandy asked, her quick feminine instinct for scandal making her ignore all the other questions.

"You're too young to know who she was and what she did, and I'm too old to care," I said.

"My daddy says the bugs are going to get everybody." Mandy repeated this prophetic piece of eschatology indifferently, as if it didn't matter.

"Your father was referring to a recent announcement by some scientists that insects are increasing alarmingly on this planet," I said. "It is my opinion that they are increasing because they are alarmed by the steady increase of human beings."

"I want a swan to get me," Mandy said. "What do you want to get you?"

I had to give this some thought. "Bear with me," I said. "It isn't easy to decide. It would be colorful and exotic to be got by a green mamba in the Taj Mahal, but my friends would say I was just showing off, and such an ending would also be out of character. I shall probably stumble over my grandson's toy train and break my neck."

Mandy, true to form, lobbed her next question over my head. "What bear?" she said.

"I didn't say anything about a bear," I said.

"You said there was a bear with you," she said, "but there isn't any." I went back over what I had said and found the bear, but ignored it. "We are getting nowhere faster than usual," I told her.

"What animal would you rather be?" was her next question. I must have been unconsciously preparing for this one.

"I have been a lot of animals," I told her, "but there are also a lot I haven't been. I was never a road hog or a snake in the grass, but I was once a news hound."

"Once my daddy brought an Elk

> ## Once my daddy brought an Elk home, but he was just a man.

home to our house for dinner," she said, "but he was just a man." She sighed, with the dark light of an old disenchantment in her eyes.

"Men hate to be called animals," I said, "but then they form lodges and luncheon clubs and call themselves animals—Elks, Moose, Eagles, Lions, and so on. Don't ask me why they come home dog-tired from stag parties and try to outfox Mama with a cock-and-bull story." I was all set to go further with this line of attack or defense, but her interest, after her fashion, had wandered back. "Why don't you want to be a road hog?" she demanded.

"Because they turn turtle, and then the bulls ride up on motorcycles and arrest them."

"Make up a nursery rhyme,"

Mandy commanded me.

I pretended to be having a hard time making up a nursery rhyme, but my anguish was rigged, for I had made one up long ago for just such an emergency, and I recited it:

*Half a mile from Haverstraw
there lived a half-wit fellow,
Half his house was brick and
red, and half was wood and
yellow;
Half the town knew half his
name but only half could spell it.
If you will sit for half an hour,
I've half a mind to tell it.*

"My daddy makes up nursery rhymes too," Mandy said. I felt sure her daddy's doggerel would top mine, and it did.

"Tell me one of them," I said, and she did.

*Hi diddle diddle, the cat and
the fiddle,
Moscow jumped over the moon.*

"That isn't a nursery rhyme," I told her. "That is political science."

"No, it isn't," Mandy said.

"Yes, it is," I said.

"No, it isn't," she said.

"Yes, it is," I said.

"No, it isn't," she said.

It was at this point, or, to be exact, sword's point, that Mandy's mother and my wife (they are not the same person) entered the room and broke into the debate.

"You mustn't say it is if Mr. Thurber says it isn't," her mother told Mandy.

"Are you two arguing again?" my wife wanted to know.

"No," I told her. "I was just explaining to Mandy that she shouldn't get her hopes up if she asks a bull on a motorcycle the way to the next town, and he says, 'Bear left at the church.' There won't be any bear there."

"Yes, there will," Mandy said.

"No, there won't," I said.

"Stop it," my wife said. "It's time to go."

We broke it up, but at the door I said to Mandy, "Next time I'll explain why the wolf is at the door. It's on account of the stork."

"There isn't any stork, if you mean babies," Mandy said. I am sure she would have explained what she meant, in simple, childish dialectic, but my wife doesn't want me to know the facts of life.

"For heaven's sake, come on!" she said, and roughly but mercifully dragged me out of there.

MORAL: If it's words that you would bandy, never tangle with a Mandy.

Our grandson's scoutmaster must have fainted when he saw what he'd texted to his troop's parents: "Scouts seven o'clock sharp at the church. We will finish up aviation, cycling, and gynecology merit badges."

That was followed by this message three minutes later: "Change of plans. We will not be finishing up the gynecology merit badge. Instead, it will be the genealogy merit badge."

— CAROL ALLISON

While we were visiting Block Island, off the New England coast, my friend, who'd had a few, called to ask me for a ride home. "I'm outside Iggi's Inn," he slurred.

After many hours— and even more miles— driving around looking for Iggi's Inn, I finally found him. He was leaning against a large sign for the 1661 Inn.

— CLAYTON LUCE

News that her third child was going to be a girl thrilled my cousin, who already had two boys. "My husband wants to call her Sunny," she told me, "and I want to give her Anna as her middle name in memory of my mom." I thought they might want to reconsider their decision, since their birth announcement would herald the arrival of Sunny Anna Rainey.

— CAROLYN WALLIS

While waiting in line at the Department of Vehicle Services for my new license plate, I heard the clerk shout out "E-I-E-I-O."

"Here," the woman standing next to me answered. Curious, I asked if she was married to a farmer, or maybe taught preschool.

"Neither," she replied. "My name is McDonald."

— JIM PIERCE

I was admiring my aunt's necklace when she surprised me by announcing, "I'm leaving it to you in my will."

I was overjoyed, perhaps too much. "Oh!" I shouted. "I'm looking forward to that!"

— MONA RANDEM

Religion is generally a verboten topic for everyone at work, except for Larry. Recently, after he steered yet another conversation toward the subject, a coworker whispered to me, "That Larry—he always has to put his two saints in."

— MARK LATESSA

"All this time I assumed it was a misprint."

My husband had just opened a printing business. He called it Alpha Thermography because he specialized in thermography, a type of raised print. One day I overheard my mom telling one of her friends, "It's called Alpha Pornography."

— JANICE SEIDNER

Learning to use a voice-recognition computer program, I was excited about the prospect of finally being able to write more accurately than I type. First I read out loud to the computer for about an hour to train it to my voice, then I opened a clean page and dictated a nursery rhyme to see the magic.

The computer recorded: "Murry fed a little clam, its fleas was bright and slow."

— CARRIE E. PITTS

My dad, a pastor, was attending a national Nazarene convention when a woman pointed to an empty seat and asked, "Is this seat saved?" Dad replied, "No, but we're praying for it."

— CHERYL STRICKLAND

Words That Should Exist

■

Hangry, a portmanteau that describes the irritability that arises from hunger, succinctly gets at a very particular human emotion. Shouldn't we have more of these terms? Here are some clever nominees.

BURALYSIS: The paralyzing anxiety you feel when confronted with bureaucracy.

PRETEDIUM: The mixture of frustration, ennui, and anxiety that washes over you when you realize you've been cornered by a known long-talker.

REMBARRASSMENT: A feeling of humiliation at the memory of an awkward or shameful experience from long ago, often unrelated to current circumstances.

CREDITPHORIA:
The pleasure, denial, delusion, and mania of being in a store you don't belong in and buying an item you cannot afford.

PREMOJI: The feeling of searching on your smartphone for an emoji that doesn't exist.

— THECUT.COM

In the British documentary 56 Up, a man shared that he had earned a law degree at Oxford. Then, in his thick English accent, he proudly proclaimed that he was now a barrister.

My 13-year-old daughter wasn't impressed. "So," she said, "he spent all that effort getting an Oxford law degree, and now he works at Starbucks?"

— LAUREN JOYCE

My nine-year-old and I passed a store with a sign that read "Watch Batteries Installed—$5."

He seemed confused: "Who would pay to watch batteries installed?"

— DEB MORRIS

We took our children to a restaurant named The Captain's Table. Our eldest wanted to go to the bathroom, but soon returned confused and embarrassed.

"Couldn't you find the way?" I asked him.

"Yes, I could," he replied, on the verge of tears, "but I don't know if I'm a buccaneer or a wench."

— TRACY FRY

When my 15-year-old son Pat stepped up to the plate during a Colt League baseball game, the young announcer declared, "Now batting, the right fielder, number 12, Pathogen!"

After some confusion in the stands, the announcer came back on over the loudspeaker. "Oh, I get it—Pat Hogan!"

— LINDA HOGAN

The first day of college can be disorienting, even for returning students. I was walking in the lobby of one of our main buildings when an upperclassman stopped me. "Excuse me," he said, looking lost. "Is the second floor still upstairs?"

— KAREN LOVE

Spelling makes a difference. I found I wasn't really interested in a recipe I discovered in our local newspaper after reading "Bigger bowels are recommended if you double this recipe."

— CAROLYN FLYNN

Timeless Humor from the '80s
■

The Army Corps of Engineers has a standard procedure for naming projects such as dams: The structure usually is designated with the name of the nearest community. One exception I know of is a dam built in my state of West Virginia. The official name of the project is the Summersville Dam, but Summersville is not the nearest town. The Corps passed over that community for obvious reasons: The town's name is Gad.

— JAMES BICKNELL

My wife walked into a coffee shop on Halloween to find the woman behind the counter with a bunch of sponges pinned to her uniform.

"I'm assuming this is a costume," said my wife. "But what are you supposed to be?"

The waitress responded proudly, "I'm self-absorbed."

— SCOTT PIPER

My friend took her teenage daughter to a new doctor for a checkup. The nurse asked her the usual questions, including if she had an STD.

"No," said the teen. "We have a Toyota."

— BARBARA GAVLICK HARTNETT

My wife is a very adventurous cook. "How does this sound?" she called out from the kitchen. "Bonito, surimi, and anchovies in a decadent, silky broth."

"Sounds delicious," I hollered back. "Is that what we're having tonight?"

"No. I'm reading from this packet of cat food."

— DAVID WELLINGS

One day when we were watching a game, my mother-in-law shrieked from the kitchen, "Jim, there's a horsefly in here!"

Not taking his eyes off the screen, he barked back, "Give it some cough syrup."

— JEFF STEWART

The road by my house was in bad condition after a rough winter. Every day I dodged potholes on the way to work. So I was relieved to see a construction crew working on the road one morning. Later, on my way home, I noticed no improvement. But

"Try double-clucking on it."

where the construction crew had been working stood a new, bright yellow sign with the words "Rough Road."

— SARAH KRAYBILL LIND

After sailing across the Atlantic, my family and I arrived in France. Wanting directions and sorely in need of conversation, my father stopped a passerby and asked if he spoke English. Sizing up my disheveled father, the man warily responded, "Sometimes."

— KATHERINE TUCKER

My mom spoke very little English. When I was going through my rebellious teenage years, I would often taunt her with the retort, "Leave me alone!"

One day, I overheard her commiserating with a friend. "All my

A man tells his doctor, "Doc, help me. I'm addicted to Twitter!"

The doctor replies, "Sorry, I don't follow you ..."

— CHRISTINA SCHRUM

daughter ever says to me is 'Give me a loan, give me a loan!'"

— KRIS KARABAN

My neighbor texted me, "I just made synonym buns!"

I texted back, "You mean like grammar used to make?"

I haven't heard from her since.

— GERALD L. LOFFREDO

I was the court stenographer the day a teenager who'd been in drug rehab came before the judge. He told the court how he was gradually overcoming his addiction. The judge was impressed. "Well done," he said. "Let's hope you end the year on a high."

— PHILIP HORTON

After purchasing lumber, I read the warning on the receipt. It confirmed what I already knew— I was happy to be married. The receipt read: "Handling may cause spinsters."

— DIANE SLAUGHTER

Our surname, Stead, rhymes with bed, but people often say steed, like the horse. One day a business associate of mine came over to the house and was greeted by my mother.

"Is Mr. Steed in?" the woman asked.

"He's Stead," my mother snapped.

"Oh, no," the woman gasped. "I was talking to him only yesterday."

— J. STEAD

like many people, I have an e-mail box that fills with junk I quickly delete. But this past May, one subject line piqued my interest: "Father's Day deals for the man who gave birth to you."

— ROB MACKEY

Once I'd finished reviewing my daughter's homework, I gave her an impromptu quiz. "What is a group of whales called?" I asked. "I'll give you a hint—it sounds like something you use to listen to music."

"An iPod?" she guessed.

"Close," I said. "But what I'm thinking of is a little smaller."

"A Shuffle!"

— GARY SELINGER

The young father took a seat on the bus next to an elderly man and plopped his one-year-old on his own lap, just as the little boy began to cry and fidget.

"That child is spoiled, isn't he?" the old man remarked.

"No," said the dad. "They all smell this way."

— ROBERT HOWE

A classified ad for a 1991 Ford Tempo recently caught my eye. The reason the car was for sale: "Mother passed away totally loaded."

— CAROL CARDALL

Who knew I lived in such a wild area? Our neighborhood newsletter published this warning: "Bikers and walkers, it is suggested you wear clothing when out after dark."

— DENNIS MULDER

My family was in a celebrating mood, so we decided to go out to a fancy steakhouse. As our waiter stood there ready to take our orders, I was caught up listening to the background music that was piped into the restaurant. "What CD is this?" I asked him.

Apparently my East Texas accent confused him, because he leaned over and answered, "Fort Worth."

— JULIE A. FOLGER

Getting through boot camp left my friend Scott feeling like a pretty big deal. So he got a vanity license plate to show exactly what he thought of himself. The plate reads: IM A STD.

— JENNIFER THIEMANN

"I think I'll just stay in tonight, maybe open a can of worms."

was waiting with my brother, Sid, at the doctor's office. When the receptionist pulled Sid's file, she noted that two files had the same name. He explained that he and his father had the same name, but that his father had passed away.

The receptionist said, "So one of you is dead and the other isn't."

"That is correct," Sid said.

"Which one are you?" she asked, pointing to the files.

"The live one, I hope!" Sid replied.

— DEBORAH STERN

regnant with my third child, I was stricken with a bout of morning sickness and lay down on the living-room couch to rest.

Just then one of the workmen who was doing repairs in my house walked by and gave me a curious look. "Taking a little break," I explained. "I'm in my first trimester."

"Really?" he said. "What's your major?"

— CARA ANDERSON

WHOEVER SAID REVENGE IS SWEET NEVER TASTED THE YUMMINESS OF FORGET-ABOUT-IT.

— **KAREN SALMANSOHN**

As far as I'm concerned, "whom" is a word that was invented to make everyone sound like a butler.

— **CALVIN TRILLIN**

Never stop worrying. Live each day as if your rent is due tomorrow.

— **CARL HIAASEN**

I always say I have a superpower. My superpower is that I'm unembarrassable.

— **TERRY CREWS**

Wearing daytime pajamas and then changing into nighttime pajamas sets a good example for your children.

— **SARAH MICHELLE GELLAR**

The way I look at it, every day that I'm moving forward is a day I'm not moving backward.

— **BOBBY BONES**

The problem with people who have no vices is that they're pretty sure to have some annoying virtues.

— **ELIZABETH TAYLOR**

As soon as women start registering a complaint, men call it nagging.

— **STEVE HARVEY**

JUST DIALED THE WRONG PERSON ON SKYPE. GUESS I MADE A SKYPO.

— **ALLEN KLEIN**

THAT HOUSEBREAKER GAVE THEM THE SLIP

The police couldn't outwit this
sneaky intruder.

By Juda Woods-Hamlin

One night in 1969, recently divorced, I was busy in the kitchen of my newly rented house while my daughters, ages five and two, slept.

I heard a noise that sounded as if the five-year-old had fallen out of bed. As I rounded the corner to check, I saw a huge snake coiled in the doorway of the girls' room.

Transfixed, I stood there until the snake slithered away, then I leapt into the room, grabbed both girls out of bed, took another leap to a coffee table, and deposited them on a couch. They were still half asleep.

I got on the phone to my mother to take the kids for the night. Then I called the police.

"I have a snake in my bedroom!"

Chuckles on the other end. "What's his name?"

Near hysteria, I managed to convince the dispatcher that I was serious. Two officers arrived and did a thorough search of the room, pulling out drawers, lifting the mattress, and poking through the closet. At one point, an officer pulled a belt from the closet and, putting a finger to his lips to warn me to be quiet, slid it along the other officer's back. The poor man jumped about three feet in the air.

They found nothing and left after an hour. Soon after, so did I.

The next morning I called my landlord, who met me at the house toting four rat traps.

"But it was a snake," I told him, "not a rat!" Despite my doubts, I got home that night to find the snake caught in the traps. Using a rake, the landlord picked it up, traps attached, and carried it outside. The thing was almost five feet long—my landlord thoughtfully mailed me a picture.

At my request, the landlord sent the snake's mugshot to the police station.

LOL

Spotting a candle in my dentist's bathroom with the helpful inscription "CALMING," I smiled cynically and thought, Oh sure. Later, as I nervously settled into the dental chair, I told my dentist his candle wasn't working. He replied, "That's for us."

— JEAN BROWN

Hamburger and fries," a man orders.

"Me too," says the ostrich sitting beside him.

"That's $9.40," the waitress says. The man reaches into his pocket and hands her exact change. They return the next day. Both order a steak and potato, and again the man pays with exact change.

"How do you do that?" the waitress asks.

"A genie granted me two wishes," explains the man. "My first was that I'd always have the right amount of money to pay for anything."

"Brilliant! But what's with the ostrich?"

"My second wish was for an exotic chick with long legs who agrees with everything I say."

— EDWARD M. JEAN

A farmer on a tractor addressed a driver whose car was stuck in a mud hole. "For ten bucks, I'll pull you out of there," the farmer said.

"All right," the driver agreed. After the farmer had pocketed the money, he said, "You know, yours is the tenth car I've rescued today."

"Wow," the driver said incredulously. "When do you have time to work on your land? At night?"

"No," the farmer replied. "Night is when I fill the hole with water."

— RODRIGO CAMARGO

My son, a used-car dealer, showed his customer a 2005 Chevy in great condition. "And it's only $7,000," he told the man.

"I'm willing to give you $3,500," said the customer.

My son feigned disappointment. "If at all possible," he responded, "I'd like to sell you the whole car."

— LIZ BROOKER

Filling out a credit card application, my friend came upon this question: "What is your source of income?" She wrote: "ATM."

— MICHAEL MCRAE

The plan: to build a garden walkway made up of dozens of wooden squares. I decided I'd slice railroad ties into two-inch-thick pieces for the sections. That's what I told the clerk at the lumber yard.

"You got a power saw?" he asked

"No," I said. "Can't I just use my hand saw?"

He nodded slowly. "You could. But I just have one question: How old do you want to be when you finish?"

— JUDY MYERS

I was at the drugstore and noticed a young male cashier staring at the pretty girl in front of me. Her total came to $14.62, and after handing over a $100 bill, she waited for change. "Here you go," said the cashier, smiling as he returned the proper amount. "Have a great day!"

On the first day of her vacation, my coworker fell and broke her leg. As the doctor examined her, she moaned, "Why couldn't this have happened on my last day of skiing?"

He looked up. "This is your last day of skiing."

— EDNA KITCHEN

Now I placed my items on the counter. The tally was $32.79, and I too gave the cashier a $100 bill. "I'm sorry, ma'am. We can't accept anything larger than a fifty," he told me, pointing to a sign stating store policy.

"But you just accepted that last girl's hundred," I reasoned.

"I had to," he said. "It had her phone number on it."

— KAREN REHM

I had signed up to be a school volunteer and was helping a first-grader with her homework. But it turned out I was the one in need of help. The assignment required coloring, and

I'm color-blind—can't tell blue from red. As we finished our lesson, I told the little girl, "Next week you can read to me."

Looking confused, she said, "Can't you read, either?"

— HOWARD SIEPLINGA

I loved the dress that I bought at a flea market. It fit perfectly, and the skirt was a swirl of intricate pleats. I wore it confidently to an evening party and glowed when a woman exclaimed, "Oh, how stunning!" Yes, I was grinning from ear to ear, until she added cheerfully, "Hang on to it, honey. Pleats will come back someday."

— MARY LOU WICKHAM

God is speaking to Moses.

God: I've got good news and bad news.

Moses: Give me the good news first.

God: The good news is that you have been chosen to deliver my people from bondage. I will force the pharaoh to free the people by sending plagues of locusts, frogs, darkness, and more. The pharaoh's armies will chase you to the Red Sea, but don't worry. I will help you part the waters to aid your escape.

Moses: So, what's the bad news?

God: You have to prepare the environmental impact statement.

— ROBERT STRAND

In an attempt to balance work and motherhood, I delegated the grocery shopping to my young babysitter. But the job proved a tad daunting.

As a retired chemist, I was interested in some unusual chemical towers at a factory. Curious, I asked a guard, "What do they make there?" He replied, "$8.35 an hour."

— ROBERT JOSLIN

One day while I was at work, she texted me from the supermarket.

"Can't find Brillo pads," she wrote. "All they have are Tampax and Kotex."

— KIMBERLY CLARK

Our day care center spent time helping the kids memorize their home addresses. My daughter, who was in my class, had her street name down, but couldn't remember the house number.

"If our house is on fire and you call 911," I asked, "how will the firefighters know where to go?"

She had a plan: "I'll tell them to go to South 14th Street and look for the house that's on fire."

— DIANNA PHYFER

The knit cap my friend sent me from England was a bit small. But it was lovely, so I wore it to church that Sunday. Afterward, I e-mailed her to say how nice it looked on me. She shot me back a note saying how glad she was. "Especially," she wrote, "since it's a tea cozy."

— JAMIE CARLSON

I opened the door on Halloween to find a superhero in our midst. Admiring his colorful outfit and mask, I asked, "Are you Spider-Man?"

Clearly concerned I'd lost it, he answered, "I'm a kid. This is a costume."

— CATHY MUMAW

One afternoon I rushed out of the house, forgetting my keys, and found myself locked out. There was nothing I could do but wait for my husband to come home, so I went over to a neighbor who was outside raking leaves.

"You locked yourself out?" he said.

"Yeah. This is the second time since we moved in. After the first time we took an extra key and put it in a jar, then stuck it in a potted plant on the back deck."

"So what's the problem?"

"I took the plants in for the winter."

— ADRIANA DESIMONE

As a high school Latin teacher, I'm used to fielding questions about my subject, which some find arcane and ancient. However, I was surprised when someone asked, "Do you have any native speakers in your class?"

Sadly, that person was the principal.

— KEITHA ITO

Turning to me with some urgency, my sleeping husband stated, "I have to do the cat's taxes!"

— CANDACE R. RENARD
STAUNTON

Standing in line in a hardware store, I noted a woman looking at a rack full of signs priced at $1.79 each. She took one out and put it back a couple of times. Suddenly she held up the sign that read "Help Wanted," and asked the clerk, "Is there a discount on the sign if it's just going over the kitchen sink?"

— DONALD GEISER

What happens when an artist has trouble finding inspiration? She draws a blank.

— CHERYL HERMAN

Timeless Humor from the '40s

■

Penny Candy! The big showcase in the tiny Iowa store was crammed with every conceivable kind. The little old proprietress, cute as a lemon drop herself, smiled as I selected some of each variety— nearly $2 worth. "I haven't had so much fun in ages," I remarked.

"You can have more fun next time," she said with a twinkle.

"How?"

"Next time, bring one penny."

— LT. (J.O.) MAX HODGE

*"... and then we'll clear the blockage
by inserting a tiny balloon."*

Concerned that he might have put on a few pounds, my husband exited the bathroom and asked, "Do you think my chin is getting fat?"

I smiled lovingly and replied, "Which one?"

— JULIE ECHELMEIER

I was browsing in the men's department at Neiman Marcus when a knitted black designer blazer caught my eye.

Although the tag said it was on sale, it still cost more than I cared to spend. Tempting fate, I tried it on. Just then, a saleswoman appeared.

"It fits you perfectly," she said.

"Yes," I said, "but I really don't need it."

Without missing a beat, she replied, "We don't sell things that people need."

— JOE CAPUTO

MY CONCESSION SPEECH

Though the election for president of his house ended in defeat, this member of the loyal opposition prefers to go out with his head held high.

By Andy Simmons

My fellow Americans, earlier this year I threw my hat into the political arena and announced my candidacy for president of our house, 347 Elm Street. My goal was simple: unseat the incumbent, my wife—Mommy, who I believed had grown careless in how she handled the affairs of our home.

I ran on a strict law-and-order platform: Finish one jar of peanut butter before opening another one. No talking to me when the Mets are batting. If you take a slice of pizza, close the box so the rest of the slices stay warm. And no matter how much whining and cajoling, we are not buying a dog.

My qualifications to take this household of three in the right direction were evident. I was and remain the only one in the family who can open pickle jars. I was and remain the only one who can remember the Amazon Prime password. I was and remain the only one who doesn't scream when he sees small bugs. I was and remain the Best Dad—see my coffee cup.

It was a close contest that saw me make many inroads during the debates, where I pressed my opponent on the hottest topics of the day. On infrastructure spending, I made a bold stand, insisting "It's not broken; you have to jiggle the handle!" On the issue of transportation, I questioned my rival's refusal to make left-hand turns. And on health care, I fought the lonely battle against buying a dog, reminding everyone "I'm allergic!"

But tonight, the votes have been cast, the ballots tallied, the people of this great house have spoken, and

I respect their decision. And while I take great pride in how close the election was—two votes to one—it is clear that I will not be your next president.

Only minutes ago, I turned to my opponent, sitting next to me on the couch, and congratulated her. She nodded graciously before raising the volume on the TV as she continued to watch another episode of *Succession*.

As contentious as this campaign has been, it is now time to unite our home around the winner. I call for all my supporters, namely myself, to fall in line to ensure a smooth transition from the previous Mommy administration to the next Mommy administration, which will mark her 21st term in office.

Although I will not be serving as your president and commander-in-chief, I will continue to fight for the things that my campaign stood for, especially that one about the peanut butter.

Now, as I prepare to end my campaign and take our new dog for a walk, I thank each and every voter, no matter whom you recklessly voted for. And may God bless 347 Elm Street.

My great-aunt looked confused when I told her that my daughter was 18 months old. "Oh," she said. "I thought she was a year and a half."

"But Aunt Marie," I said, "18 months and a year and a half are the same."

She shrugged. "What do I know? I never had kids."

— JOEL BRILL

When I press my forehead with my finger, it really hurts," a patient complained to his doctor. "And when I do the same to my cheek, it's also painful. Even if I press on my stomach, I suffer. What can it be?"

Stumped, the physician sent the patient to a specialist. The man returned to his doctor the following week.

"What did the specialist say?" the doctor asked.

"I have a broken finger."

— GEORGE RUSSELL

The local wholesale warehouse sells everything from tires to tuna fish. I was there around noon and stopped at the lunch counter for a slice of pizza. I ate only half of it and threw my leftovers in a nearby trashcan.

Then I turned to see a man standing there, hot dog in one hand, ketchup in the other, with a look of horror on his face. I asked him what was wrong. He said, "I just purchased that trash can!"

— CHRIS BIRCH

Feeling sick, my sister grabbed the thermometer from the medicine cabinet and popped it into her mouth.

"Uh, Julie, that's the dog's thermometer," said my mother.

Julie spit out the thermometer. "Ew, that was in Fitzie's mouth?"

Mom hesitated before replying, "Not exactly."

— JANET GALLO

During a home renovation, my grandfather was watching me drive in nails. "You hammer like lightning," he said.

"Really?" I replied, flattered.

"You never strike the same place twice."

— DAVE LOCKETT

Having avoided the scale for a few years, my husband finally got up the nerve to climb aboard. Unable to read the numbers, he got off to grab his eyeglasses and stepped back on.

"What do you know?" he called out. "These glasses weigh 50 pounds."

— ERMA THOMPSON

"Do you think it's wise to move away from solar energy?"

I **was trapped** in an elevator for 30 minutes before the doors finally opened. Relieved, I said to a fellow hostage, "There's a first time for everything."

She grumbled back, "There's a last time for everything too."

— CAROL LEISH

S **uffering from** an unsightly scaly rash, my friend Denise made an appointment with a dermatologist who happened to be very attractive.

After a full examination, the doctor cocked his head and asked, "Denise, did you get your hair done?"

"Why, yes. Thank you for noticing," said Denise, flattered.

"I thought so," the doctor replied. "Because your scalp looks red and irritated."

— SANDY HAGGLUND

You've gotta help me," a man said to a psychiatrist. "Every night this week I've dreamed I'm playing in a badminton tournament. Then I wake up tired and sweaty."

"OK, here's your medicine," the doctor said. "Drink this right away, and you'll be cured in no time.

"Can't I wait and drink it tomorrow?" the dreamer wanted to know.

"Why?" the doctor asked.

"Tonight is our championship game."

— EMILY LEYBLE

t the DMV to renew her license, my mother had her photo taken and waited for her new card. Finally her name was called and she went to the counter to pick it up.

"Good grief," she said. "My picture's hideous. It looks nothing like me."

The woman in line behind her plucked it out of her hand. "That's because it's mine."

— CLARE SPAULDING

IAN BAKER.

During a storm, my wife's car became stuck in a snowbank. Our obstetrician saw her spinning her wheels, trying to get out. When he offered to help, my wife could not resist telling him, "OK, Doctor. When I count to three, push!"

— H. STEINBERG

A man is woken up by a knock at the door one morning. He gets up and goes downstairs to open the door and is met by a six-foot-six-inch spider who immediately head-butts him, runs inside, tramples all over the man, kicks him in the back, boots his ribs, and stamps all over him.

The next thing the homeowner remembers is waking up in hospital. Turning to the doctor he says, "I feel terrible. What's wrong with me?"

"Don't worry, everything's all right,"

A priest, a nun, a rabbi, a lawyer, and a doctor walk into a bar. The bartender takes one look at them and says, "What is this? A joke?"

— SEAN MORRISON

the doctor tells him. "It's just a vicious bug going about."

— PHIL MURPHY

Purpose of visit?" asked the customs agent as we approached a checkpoint at the Canada-U.S. border.

"We're going to a wedding," my wife said. "Are you carrying any weapons—knives, guns?" he asked.

"No," she said. "It's not that kind of wedding."

— MARTIN JAGODZINSKI

Looking out a diner window, I noticed a woman struggling to parallel park. After a few minutes of watching her inch up, inch back, inch out, and inch in, I

went outside to offer my help, which she readily accepted. After I parked her car, a man came over to thank me. "You're welcome," I said. "Are you her husband?"

"No," he replied. "I'm the guy parked behind her."

— MITCHELL PLANTIER

I live for baseball. But I had to go to work during an important game, so I asked my wife to tape it for me. After I left the office, I flew through our front door, bursting with anticipation.

"Don't tell me the score!" I yelled to her.

"I don't know the score," she assured me. "All I know is that your team lost."

— MICHAEL BOGGESS

While sightseeing at George Washington's home in Mount Vernon, Virginia, a family friend became nervous when she thought she had lost two of my cousins. She looked everywhere and called out their names repeatedly. Soon our friend grew perturbed that not one of the Mount Vernon employees had joined in the search. Instead, they simply stood around, staring at her as if she were crazy. Finally, just a few moments later, my cousins—George and Martha—came out from hiding.

— TRACY NELSON

Dad's a safety-first kind of guy. But while vacationing with some buddies, he was talked into going parasailing. He was on the back of the boat getting hooked into the parachute when he nervously asked the pilot, "How often do you replace the rope?"

The pilot replied, "Every time it breaks."

— MICHAEL WASMER

With a new book on handwriting analysis, I began practicing on colleagues at work. One skeptical woman asked if she could bring in a sample of her daughter's writing. "Of course," I replied.

Next day, the woman handed me an envelope. I opened it, read the contents, then dramatically told her, "Your daughter is 14 years old. She's an A student. She loves music and horses."

Amazed, the woman ran off to tell her friends before I could show her the note. It read: "I'm 14 years old and an A student. I love music and horses. My mother thinks you're a fake."

— BILL WHITMAN

I was talking to my doctor about a weight-loss patch I had seen advertised. Supposedly you stick it on and the pounds melt away. "Does it work?" I asked.

"Sure," he said. "If you put it over your mouth."

— MARY KAAPKE

I've never wanted to know the answer to anything bad enough to ask a question at a meeting that's running 30 minutes over time.

— @ABBYHASISSUES (ABBY HEUGEL)

"Remember No Child Left Behind? Well, obviously, the bus driver doesn't."

Vacationing in Hawaii, two priests decide to wear casual clothes so they won't be identified as clergy. They buy Hawaiian shirts and sandals, and soon hit the beach. They notice a gorgeous blonde in a tiny bikini.

"Good afternoon, Fathers," she says as she strolls by.

The men are stunned. How does she know they're clergy? They buy even wilder attire: surfer shorts, tie-dyed T-shirts, and dark glasses.

The next day, they return to the beach. The same fabulous blonde, now wearing a string bikini, passes by, nods politely at them, and says, "Good morning, Fathers."

"Just a minute, young lady," says one of the priests. "We are priests and proud of it, but how in the world did you know?"

"Don't you recognize me? I'm Sister Kathryn from the convent."

— **MICHAEL RANA**

"Every year I say 'Just a little off the top,'
but they never listen !"

A **young** American tourist goes on a guided tour of a creepy old castle in England. "How did you enjoy it?" the guide asked when it was over.

"It was great," the girl replied, "but I was afraid I was going to see a ghost in some of those dark passageways."

"No need to worry," said the guide. "I've never seen a ghost in all the time I've been here."

"How long is that?" she asked.

"About 300 years."

— **DONALD GEISER**

O **ne of** the players on our junior high football team never saw action in a game. But my brother, the assistant coach, liked the kid and always gave him pep talks.

"Remember, Ben," he told him, "everyone on this team has an

important role. There is no I in team."

"True," said the boy. "But there is a Ben in bench."

— ALICIA ELLEY

Gonna update my CV to say "survived 1,000 Zoom calls that should've been an e-mail" as part of my achievements in 2020.

— @ALANAH_TORRALBA

My mother lacks a green thumb, but she keeps at it.

Pointing one day to a line of new plants by the kitchen window, my sister whispered to me, "Look—death row."

— MICHAEL KNIGGE

While getting dressed one morning, I decided I'd been spending too much time on my computer: I caught myself checking the lower right corner of my makeup mirror to see what time it was.

— DARLENE JACOBS

Freelance newspaper writers don't get nearly as much attention as writers with regular bylines. So I was delighted when I finally got some notice. It was at the bank, and I was depositing a stack of checks.

"Wow," said the teller, reading off the names of publishers from the tops of the checks. "You must deliver a lot of papers."

— MEGAN FRANCIS

Apparently I tend to brag too much about my home state of Ohio. One day I told a long-suffering friend, "You know, the first man in powered flight was from Ohio. The first man to orbit the earth was from Ohio. And the first man on the moon was from Ohio."

"Sounds like a lot of people are trying to get out of Ohio."

— JEAN NEIDHARDT

Timeless Humor from the '70s

■

While hitchhiking through a western state, a friend and I went into a small-town store. The clerk, noticing our unkempt appearance and shabby attire, politely asked us to leave. Trying to get out of the situation, I said in my best high school French, "*Je ne parle pas l'anglais.*"

After studying me for a few moments, she said, "Yeah? Well, your French ain't none too good either."

— J. JANELLE MASTERS

Friends of ours from Maine, Sam and Ruth, had just bought a car when winter hit with all its fury. "I wonder if the car has seat warmers," Ruth wondered.

"It does," said Sam, looking through the owner's manual. "Here it is: rear defrosters."

— DALE DUTTON

During a summer-camp sing-along around the campfire, I grabbed my guitar and accompanied the kids. After five or six songs, I asked, "OK, what should we sing next?"

One ten-year-old requested, "A cappella."

—GEORGE HEROUX

Our fourth grader celebrated his birthday on crutches, so he couldn't carry the cupcakes into school without help. I asked our sixth grader, Noah, to help his brother carry them in.

"I could," he said, "but I'd prefer not to."

Spotting a teaching moment, my husband asked Noah, "What would Jesus do?"

Noah answered, "Jesus would heal him so he could carry his own cupcakes."

— RACHEL NICHOLS

My grandmother has lived all her 80 years in northern New England, where what she sees from November until April is mostly snow. When my husband and I moved to California in January, we couldn't wait to phone and tell her about our green lawns, green trees, and flowers that bloom all winter long.

My nephew gave up his lucrative job to become a writer. "Have you sold anything yet?" I asked him one day.

"Yes," he said. "My car and my television."

— PATRICK DICKINSON

"It sounds lovely, dear," she replied. "But doesn't it look terribly artificial?"

— MARGARET HEAGY

My wife and I decided we'll need a vacation once the world reopens. I taped a world map to the refrigerator, gave my wife a magnetic dart, and said, "Wherever it lands is our vacation spot!"

Seems we'll be spending two weeks behind the fridge.

— JOSEPH HUBISZ

The worst part of stopping during a road trip is knowing all the idiots you've passed are once again getting ahead of you.

— @CARBOSLY

TODAY ME WILL LIVE IN THE MOMENT. UNLESS IT IS UNPLEASANT. IN WHICH CASE ME WILL EAT A COOKIE.

— COOKIE MONSTER

People can't drive you crazy if you don't give them the keys.

— MIKE BECHTLE

My grandmother started walking five miles a day when she was 60. She's 97 now and we don't know where the hell she is.

— ELLEN DEGENERES

Life is too short to miss out on the beautiful things, like a double cheeseburger.

— CHANNING TATUM

Next time you are discussing an important issue with someone, ask yourself, Is this a monologue or a dialogue? Personally, I'm only interested in the latter.

— REESE WITHERSPOON

I decided to learn to play the drums, which is the best medicine. For me, at least— maybe not so much for those around me.

— BUBBA WALLACE

I would never name-drop. It's tacky. My best friend, Gwyneth Paltrow, taught me that.

— ROSS MATHEWS

I have a confidence now that comes from a combination of years of experience and not caring anymore.

— ALTON BROWN

I NEVER SING IN THE SHOWER. IT'S VERY DANGEROUS.

— JIMMY FALLON

SHE SAW RED AND LOST IT

That story was a bit too juicy.

By Maureen King Cassidy

My husband and I moved from the New York City metro area in the 1980s to Pennsylvania, a location that was quieter and more affordable.

While in New York, I'd worked as a local radio news reporter. That experience helped me land a job as a TV news anchor in a semirural area of my new state.

One night, when my coanchor and I were delivering the evening news on air, I had to read a story about a local resident who had grown a very large tomato.

As I read the teleprompter on live TV, I was struck unexpectedly by the humor of an oversize vegetable being newsworthy enough to make it on local TV. (Of course, it would never happen in New York.)

When the featured tomato loomed up on the screen like a gigantic blood moon, I started laughing. Things only got worse as the segment continued, with a reporter at the scene interviewing the grower, treating the story with due sincerity in an area of the country where gardening is serious business.

"How long did it take to grow it this big?" the reporter asked. "Did you use any special methods to achieve that?"

My laughing was beyond control at this point. I barely got through the rest of the segment.

But the story and its peculiarities didn't stop there. The night after our news piece aired, someone stole the giant tomato from the woman's yard. Then, in an even stranger twist, the prized vegetable was returned the next day.

I learned in the follow-up that the gardener was not happy after she saw the footage of me laughing at her unusual accomplishment.

It wasn't one of my finer moments as a broadcaster, but it's a news story I will never forget.

ALSO AVAILABLE
FROM READER'S DIGEST

Dumb Dad Jokes

A collection of riddles, jokes, one-liners, hilarious anecdotes, and pointed wit about dads and families: our chief source of amusement.

ISBN 978-1-62145-430-4
$9.99 paperback

Laughter Totally Is the Best Medicine

More than 1,000 of the funniest quips, quotes, anecdotes, and cartoons from *Reader's Digest* magazine—just what the doctor ordered.

ISBN 978-1-62145-406-9
$9.99 paperback

Fun Jokes for Funny Kids, Volume 2

A jam-packed compilation of knock-knock jokes, ridiculous riddles, and perfect puns guaranteed to keep kids from ages 6 to 106 rolling in laughter.

ISBN 978-1-62145-451-9
$6.99 paperback

For more information, visit us at RDTradePublishing.com
E-book editions are also available.

Reader's Digest books can be purchased through
retail and online bookstores.